John Ernest Merrill

Ideals and Institutions Their Parallel Development

John Ernest Merrill

Ideals and Institutions Their Parallel Development

ISBN/EAN: 9783337064402

Printed in Europe, USA, Canada, Australia, Japan

Cover: Foto ©Thomas Meinert / pixelio.de

More available books at **www.hansebooks.com**

IDEALS AND INSTITUTIONS

THEIR PARALLEL DEVELOPMENT

*A Thesis presented at the University of
Minnesota for the Degree of
Doctor of Philosophy*

BY

JOHN ERNEST MERRILL, B.A.

Hartford Seminary Press
HARTFORD, CONN.
1894

Copyright, 1894, by
JOHN ERNEST MERRILL

The Case, Lockwood & Brainard Co., Printers, Hartford, Conn.

PREFACE

The following pages contain a presentation of some historical bearings of the theory of the moral ideal. One of their results is to bring to that theory the weight of an historical confirmation.

Part I is intended as the metaphysical basis for and introduction to the historical study which occupies Part II.

The paragraph entitled Causality, at the close of each section in Part II, is intended simply to point out the causality of the ideal in the development of the institution in hand. While this is a matter of no little interest and importance, its exhibition is not the main object of the thesis' argument, whence the skeleton-like form of statement, and the smaller type.

Obviously, the most difficult problem has been the ascertainment of the ideal. In the later ages, and in some of the earlier, there is literary material of the times from which we get a tolerably clear idea. But in other cases, the method is, of necessity, one of insight. The ideal inferred from a single institution, finding verification as the ideal of an age, when applied as such to that age's other institutions, has thus an historical presumption established in its favor. And if it coördinates in an historical development with the ideals of other ages, obtained by a similar method, or more especially with those revealed in literature of the times, the ideal may be regarded as substantially correct.

In reading Part II, it will be of value to keep in mind the development of any single institution as a whole. Otherwise the presentation of its early stages, as its original, and for us basal form, its point of departure, will seem little else than a rehearsal of facts of common knowledge. It will be helpful, also, to have well fixed in mind the course of development of the ideal as one follows the development of the corresponding institutions. In both these matters, the paragraphs entitled CAUSALITY and the charts at the end of each chapter may render assistance.

Appended is a list of the authorities which have been consulted, in part or in whole, in the preparation of the thesis. Especial indebtedness should be acknowledged to the last chapter of Schurman's "Ethical Import of Darwinism" for its suggestiveness in the early consideration of the general subject, to Green's "Prolegomena to Ethics," to Andrews' "Institutes of General History," and to Wilson's "The State"; also to various persons who have given helpful criticism, and to Professor Williston S. Hough, in charge of the Department of Philosophy.

JOHN ERNEST MERRILL

November 23, 1894

TABLE OF CONTENTS

	Page
Preface	5
Table of Contents	7
Thesis	9

PART I: METAPHYSICAL

Chapter I: The Ideal 13–24
    Introductory; Basis of Moral Theory, End of Conduct
    Definitions of the Ideal, with consideration of objections
    Development of the Ideal
    Racial and National Ideals

Chapter II: Institutions . 25–30
    Definitions
    Sanctions and Causes of Institutions
    Change in Institutions
    Classification of Institutions

Chapter III: Static Relation of Ideals and Institutions. Their Correspondence 31–35
    Introductory
    Institutions from the point of view of the Ideal
    The Ideal from the point of view of Institutions
    Institutions and the Ideal constitute one whole
    Objections considered

Chapter IV: The Parallel Development of Ideals and Institutions 36–38
    Proofs and Objections
    Development is always progress
    Direction of Progress

Chapter V: Dynamic Relation of Ideals and Institutions. Priority and Causality of Ideals 39–41
    Introductory
    Priority
    Causality

PART II: HISTORICAL

Chapter I: Parallel Development of Greek Ideals and Institutions 45–72
    Preliminary
    Development of the Ideal
    Parallel Development of Institutions relating to Subjugation of Nature, Social Organization, and Individual Culture
    Other Parallel Developments
    Chart

Chapter II: Parallel Development of Roman Ideals and Institutions 73–113
    Development of the Ideal
    Parallel Development of Institutions relating to Subjugation of Nature, Social Organization, and Individual Culture
    Chart

Chapter III: Parallel Development of Ideals and Institutions in the Roman World 114–132
    Preliminary; Influence of Greece on Rome
    Development of the Ideal
    Parallel Development of Institutions relating to Subjugation of Nature and Social Organization
    Chart

Chapter IV: Parallel Development of Teutonic Ideals and Institutions 133–172
    Preliminary
    Development of the Ideal
    Parallel Development of Institutions relating to Subjugation of Nature, Social Organization, and Individual Culture
    Chart

Conclusion 173
List of Authorities 174–175

THESIS

HISTORY SHOWS A PARALLEL DEVELOPMENT OF INSTITUTIONS AND THE MORAL IDEAL.

IN THIS DEVELOPMENT, THE IDEAL HAS BEEN PRIOR TO AND CAUSALLY CONNECTED WITH ITS CORRESPONDING INSTITUTIONS.

"The great motors of the race are moral, not intellectual"

JAMES RUSSELL LOWELL

PART I

METAPHYSICAL

Chapter I

THE IDEAL

In the solution of any problem, or the development of any truth, there are always certain considerations which, while not themselves directly the matter of investigation, are so vitally connected with the subject in hand that their early study becomes a necessity. Thus, doubtless the meaning of the terms "ideal" and "institution" is popularly understood, in a general way, and perhaps not a few are aware of their peculiar ethical signification. Yet it will not be unwise for us to analyze them each quite carefully, in order that we may be sure of their exact connotation.

Any true system of morality or of ethical teaching must ultimately rest, of course, upon facts which are common to human nature. And more than this, it must be founded upon characteristics which belong to all men as such; it must find its abiding basis in the inherent character of humanity. What this foundation is, a short process of elimination will discover.

<small>Introductory— Basis of Moral Theory</small>

All men have physical bodies and exercise the functions of life. Their every activity is a manifestation that they are physically alive. But in this they do not differ essentially from the animals. In fact, the difference is not so much one of function as of structure, and in both structure and function animals are more widely separated from each other than some of them are from man.

Again, in the higher field of intellect, all men have minds and perform certain mental operations which are proof of their powers of reasoning. Yet here, two difficulties present themselves. In the first place, animals seem in a measure to join in this (when, however, it comes to abstract reasoning, we do not find them able to accompany us), and in the second, the highest and lowest degrees of mental ability in man are so far apart that a single intellectual criterion cannot be the basis of an universal morality. Wherever the standard may be placed, it is too high for some and too low for others. It cannot meet the conditions of including only persons and yet fully including all persons. What we find true of cognition and mental processes as such is true also of feeling. On the one hand, animals share with us the capacity for emotion, though we cannot posit for them what we know as the higher spiritual joys, and on the other, in matters of feeling, men are not on an equality with one another. For we know how some have warm and passionate natures, and others are very phlegmatic. Thus, although all men, and that to the exclusion of animals, can grasp abstract ideas, and though they can experience the higher feelings of happiness and joy, neither mind nor feeling *per se* is fitted to serve as a basis for morality.

And what of the will? Here again, at first sight, the animals seem to be sharers with man, and in many instances to choose to do certain things — at any rate, they differentiate between objects which are set before them, and take one in preference to the other. However, animal and human choices are not identical. This is no place, nor is there time or need for a discussion of animal consciousness and instinct or of the doctrine of Free-Will. Suffice it for our present purpose to say — what will readily be received — that human choices are distinguished by the fact that they are related to objects which are desired by the subject, whose attainment by himself he wills, objects which he conceives himself as attaining. The animal takes things as they are presented to him; man, however, as he acts has in view an end, the attainment by himself of some object. And it is upon the existence of such a conception in man, upon the fact of human self-consciousness, that human volition rests. Nor is there a differentiation here between man and man; all are on an equality. Every individual must and does make choices continually, and each choice is such without reference either to the loftiness of knowledge or to the variableness of feeling — although the three together are necessary to constitute the whole of an act of will. Thus while a capacity of no animal, self-consciousness is yet characteristic of every man. As the only capacity peculiar to him and yet universally active in him, it must be the ultimate foundation of any theory of moral action.

Settling thus on self-consciousness as the necessary basis of moral theory, we next inquire what is the end of conduct, for that is the fundamental question of all ethical study. Many men have attempted various answers. Some have been optimistic, some pessimistic; some based on theology, some on the results of physical science; some have been dogmatic and some skeptical, and a very few have been critical. But there in one solution which is competent to cover every particular case. That a man always acts to satisfy some desire will be generally admitted; he never chooses to do that to which he is not prompted by some longing. The end, the good, may therefore be generically defined as the satisfaction of desire. *End of Conduct*

But in the whole of every man's life there is one predominant end; his entire energy is concentrated upon the production of some single result. He has one primary object of desire to which all appetites and desires of the moment are compelled to become subordinate. What is it? It is, to be sure, the satisfaction of desire, but what does this formal answer signify? In short, to put the central question, does a man will the possession of things or the performance of deeds? Obviously the latter, for no *object* can give satisfaction. A man is satisfied, not when he has what he has been seeking, for by common experience he then desires something more, but when he is obtaining the object of his desire. It is not the thing itself, but its attainment, the necessary life and conduct, that can satisfy. Not the having of objects, but their attainment is the end. And so it is that man wills the realization of a self conceived by him as doing certain things; he wills the fulfillment of an ideal of himself. At this he aims. In its general direction, according to the Socratic teaching, he does all his moral walking. And with the fulfilment of this ideal there goes hand in hand the progressive satisfaction of his desire.

In a general way this sets forth the nature of the moral ideal; but we seek a more particular definition. T. H. Green is the chief representative of the theory, and it is to him that we therefore turn. From his "Prolegomena to Ethics" we get the statement, "The moral ideal is an active idea of common good."[1] The definition will bear considerable expansion. *Definitions of the Ideal — Definition from Green*

---

[1] These are not Green's words, but rather a crystallization of what he writes, Prolegomena, p. 219.

1. The ideal is first an idea. This accords with the supremacy of reason in man. Yet we should bear it prominently in mind that, as we have already noted, the reason is only a part of human nature. Green exhibits in turn the relations of intellect and desire, desire and will, and intellect and will, and then lays great emphasis on the fact that such a distinction is only logical.[1] In the individual, all the faculties are massed together, acting and reacting upon each other. So the ideal is primarily an idea, but this does not fully describe it. Desire and will each have their part, and the ideal bears peculiar marks which distinguish it from the simple idea.

2. For it is next an idea of the good, of that which satisfies desire. This satisfaction of desire is, as we have seen, the unvarying characteristic of the good. However, it aside, the objects of desire seem as many as men themselves. Yet we may distinguish by the professed objects of their desire two classes of people, those who in their thought identify the good and good things, and those who identify the good with good character. The fallacy of the quest of good things has been already hinted at, but in ordinary life this is not so apparent as might perhaps be expected. No doubt there are many who are led astray by the former of these two ideas, by the glitter of the things which appear; and they plunge into various undertakings which, by common report, will "bring a return." But as satisfying desire, it is impossible that the good should be a thing, a stationary end at which one may aim. The ideal and its manifestation must be of a similar character. The form of the manifestation and of the ideal must be of one kind. As the ideal of the sculptor, from the nature of his work, must be a physical shape — though expressing certain other things — so the ideal of the moral agent, like its manifestation, must be a life. The true identity is of the good and good character, or, in its manifestation, the good life.

3. The ideal, which is an idea of good, is an idea of common good. And it must be this. For man is by nature a social animal, and the formulation of the end must be in terms of his nature. The theory which rests on his personality as self-conscious cannot reject that personality as also social.

---

[1] Green: *Ibid.*, Book II, Chap. 2.

One brushes against his fellows every day. His continued existence is dependent more or less upon their effort. Their lives are inextricably interwoven with his. And if he should seriously attempt to plan his life so as to leave them completely out of account, not only would he find it impossible, but his own activity would be greatly hampered by any movement in that direction. The fact remains that men are in social relations, that "no man liveth unto himself"; and the ideal must, therefore, be an ideal of common good.

4. The ideal is, further, an active idea of common good. Owing to this is its peculiar function as the guide of conduct. Ideas of common good are as thick as leaves in Vallambrosa. There are, for instance, our "castles in the air" and our plans that we never even begin to realize; there are the Utopias of the poets and the social philosophers, and the — to many — visionary schemes of the communists and socialists. But for each man, there is one idea of the good — he may call it his "permanent purpose" or his "predominant end" — which we can designate as active. This is the idea by which he regulates his action, and to which, as nearly as possible, he makes his conduct correspond, the idea which is at once the cause and the goal of his activity, to whose fulfillment he bends all his energy. It is his ideal.

The moral ideal is, thus, an idea of the good, an idea of common good, and an active idea of common good.

Some further characteristics of the ideal are brought to light by another definition which seems to us to contain some truth: The moral ideal is the incarnation in idea of those principles of action which are considered morally ideal. It is true that the good is, in the ultimate analysis, the ground of morality. But principles of action, based to be sure on the nature of the good, are commonly in men's minds in deciding specific cases. And it is from this point of view, *viz.:* of principles of action, that they attempt to formulate their ideal.[1]

A Second Definition

1. It is worth while to notice in the first place that, when they do this, they possess at once the necessary thought of the ideal as enjoining activity, of which we have just been speaking in connection with the previous definition. For moral rules

---

[1] Muirhead sets forth a similar theory. Elements of Ethics, page 64, paragraph 27.

and principles have no other purpose than the guidance of conduct. They exist on the supposition that a man will do something, and their business is to direct him how to act, both at all times and in particular cases. So it is that the ideal *commands* action according to those principles of action which are considered morally ideal.

2. The definition of the ideal as an incarnation in idea answers also to the form of our common recognition of moral command and moral inspiration. Their source, we readily perceive, is an ideal of myself as doing certain things. I have before my mind a sort of incarnation of the principles of morality. This is my ideal man and I try to be like him.[1] It may be that, philosophically speaking, such imitation is rather a low sort of action. Most probably the feeling against it arises from our common observation of people who copy appearances, while lacking the reality which these should express. But the objection is here not a vital one, as we shall presently see.

3. Beyond what has been said, we further remark (*a*) that our definition thoroughly agrees with the organic unity of the moral life, and (*b*) that it emphasizes the fact that morality is first individual. In regard to the former, the moral life does not follow one rule here and another there; but, all through, it is one on the basis of a mutually agreeing set of principles. In harmony with this is the thought of the ideal as an incarnation. With respect to the latter, society is a whole, but it exists through individual action; and the ideal commands, not activity on the part of society, but social action on the part of individuals. To this, likewise, the idea of incarnation adds emphasis, for by no possibility could such a formulation be of society, or include in itself more than a single person.

There are certain considerations, more or less weighty, which may be urged against this definition.

Objections to this Definition
In the first place, the thought of a picture or form of any kind, the incarnation of certain principles, is rather materialistic. The error of thinking that this is the case arises, of course, from the use of the word "incarnation"; but if it be noted that it is an "incarnation in idea," the difficulty will be ob-

---

[1] Similarly Green, *ibid.*, p. 205. "By a moral ideal we mean some type of man or character or personal activity considered as an end in itself."

viated. To be sure, incarnation means, literally, embodiment; but it does not necessarily refer to some particular shape and form. Instead, it directs attention to those general features of nature rather than physique which characterize humanity. It calls on us to think of various characteristics under the general notion of man. And we need to put alongside our objection to this form of statement, the fact that many rules of high morality fail to affect men's lives, because of their abstraction and unreality. Men say they cannot conceive themselves, or any real man, as acting in accord with them.

Again, some one may suggest that we are making the ideal an imagination. Right — though not in the way the criticism is intended. The reason why we are accustomed to decry imaginations and to call them vain is that they are commonly thought of as not founded upon, or as contrary to, fact and principle. In some way, we have come to confine the word exclusively to this signification, but without sufficient reason. Though based on facts and principles, creations of the mind are still imaginations. So this ideal is an imaging of myself as acting according to principles of action, those principles which are considered morally ideal — but it is not a vain imagination.

A more serious objection is that to which we have already alluded, that this definition would make the moral life one of imitation, with the implication that it would lack self-determination. But by education we are all mimics. We do from our early days what we see others do; in fact, we are taught to be like them. In process of time, however, one notices in the growing boy or girl the development of individuality. His selfhood appears, both in what he says and in what he does. Are we to say that the fundamental characteristic of conduct has changed, or that there has been a change in the pattern? It would seem the latter. Personality cannot have come in as a new factor. What we notice is its development, and this means that self-consciousness has been present in the imitation of earlier examples, as well as of later ones; only in the latter, it is present in greater power. The crude ideal of the child is almost entirely external; it is the father or the mother, or some other older person. As he grows up, it assumes a more inward form. He adds to it certain factors which are not present in the father or the mother. He copies from his playmates, he acquires new ideas of life from what he reads or hears read; and so the pattern of his life becomes a more and more heterogeneous combination, involving elements from all his surroundings. This complex example, so far as he considers it as such, is his ideal of action. When he begins to reason about conduct, the ideal is compelled to assume a more consistent form. Yet, in any case, it is the sort of a man he would be. In two extreme instances we find the manifestation of this. The little boy wants to be a man just like his father. The Christian man makes confession of his aim to be like Jesus Christ. And all men in ordinary business, and in scholarly pursuits, know those who are to a large extent the living incarnations of their ideal, and whom they endeavor to imitate.

We may note, too, that this definition is in most close accord with the language of the religious life. We instinctively recall such phrases as, "And be ye imitators of God." The subject of Thomas á Kempis' book also suggests itself, "The Imitation of Christ." And beyond these, we remember that the ideal of moral perfection which Christianity presents is the center of its peculiar power as an ethical system.

Another objection may be that this definition would make the ideal definite and clearly understood, while, as a matter of fact, we know only its general direction. Certain of the roadway to the country which we seek, we are yet in truth unable clearly and fully to describe it. But as the incarnation of principles, its definiteness is exactly equal to our moral insight. The clearness of the outline of the ideal, and the distinctness of our division between right and wrong is exactly correspondent to our knowledge. The ideal is definite just in proportion as it leads one to unite himself with specific desires, as means to its fulfillment.

Since the basis of the moral ideal is man's peculiar nature as a self-conscious being, it follows that every man has a moral ideal, such in kind as that the definition of which we have been outlining.

General Objection to Theory of the Ideal

For it is a part of his nature, the moral side of his self-consciousness. Many men, however, do not confess the possession of any such ideal; in fact, they say their conduct is guided in other ways. Some seek pleasure in what they do, some act according to utilitarian considerations, and some are guided by an intuitive knowledge of right and wrong, while others aim at the greatest length, breadth, and depth of life, and still others control everything by the inexorable commands of right reason. These are not to be thought so many arguments against our theory, though they might seem so at first sight, for in their final analysis, all of them are but forms of the ideal. Man pictures himself as obtaining satisfaction, as ideally good, when he is happy or when he is gaining what is to his advantage, when he is obeying the moral intuitions of his nature, or when he is following the rigid mandate of Practical Reason. But in any case, he is attempting to fulfill his ideal, he is trying to be like his ideal man.

Aside from these philosophers, however, there are multitudes who do not formulate the object of their search. True, all men are philosophers, yet some more than others. But we cannot, on account of difference in ability in these matters, deny to them any ideal. All of us, as men and women, are human beings, self-conscious persons; and whether we are conscious of the ideal in this one form or not, the main-spring of our action is some moral ideal.

So much for the ideal itself. Every man has an ideal of conduct which guides and controls his action; he may be conscious of it as such or not. And the ideal may be. defined, proximately, as the incarnation in idea of those principles of action which are considered morally ideal; or ultimately, as an "active idea of common good." Summary Statement

We may now pass to other considerations. To justify the stating of such a thesis as ours, the ideal should develop, but does not what we have said preclude this? Is not the ideal, once and for all, the incarnation of moral principles? Yes, and No. There is a difference between the eternal Incarnation of those principles — at once the Cause and Goal of our development — and our realization of that Incarnation, the degree to which the totality of moral principles is embodied in our ideal. Mankind is not only self-conscious, but progressively so. He does not know so much of himself or of his surroundings to-day as he will to-morrow, and yesterday he knew far less. The progress which occurs, and which we can observe, in any single Development of the Ideal — Possible science is present in every realm of knowledge; and the idea of a progressive development of the ideal is as much a necessity of our nature as finite as is the presence of the ideal of our nature as self-conscious.

There are two directions in which this development of the ideal may take place. There will be, first, a development of its content. As one grows older, he finds new spheres for the discharge of moral duties. What is commonly called his standard of morality changes. It may rise to demand the most complete self-sacrifice, or it may fix upon the fulfilment of a small circle of duties, accompanied by the fullest attainment of animal pleasure. It is certain that it will include an increasing number of duties, and that the old duties will take on new meanings and will involve readjustments of life. In the morally well-balanced man, other things being equal, the direction of movement will be away from "goods of the body" toward the "goods of the soul." But individual idiosyncrasies make a general statement untrustworthy. The only thing that we can certainly maintain is the fact of development; though relatively perhaps only change, it is absolute progress. Moral stagnation and death are practically synonymous.

<small>Directions of Development</small>

There will also, very likely, be a development in the range of the ideal, though this is not so certain to appear. A few, doubtless, will ever make the aristocratic distinction on some basis or other. Yet this is to-day changing. The number of those who include in society, not simply a social clique or a local division, is constantly increasing. People are coming to believe that races are social units, and that even the peoples of the earth form one society.

In both of these lines, in the range and in the content of the ideal, there may be development; there must be continually in one. And for the majority of people the development takes place most markedly in the content of the ideal, since it is more closely connected with the duties of everyday life.

The question how ideals change, and what are the forces behind the development, though it does not directly concern our discussion, merits a brief reply. Incidentally, this calls up the relation between ideals and ideas. And we observe that

<small>Manner of Development</small>

it is by the addition of ideas that ideals are changed. For the ideal is an active idea of common good. It is not simple, but complex, including all the ranges of our action; and every idea of common good which approves itself to us, which we believe really worthy of realization by us, we make a part of our ideal. This is the process by which we come to see more and more of the ideal, by which its definition grows clearer and clearer. New ideas come with wider knowledge and truer insight, and the ideal develops by the incorporation of some of these ideas.

But the great controversy is over the influence of heredity and surroundings on character and conduct. Now, no one will claim that they are without effect, and that effect may be great; but we hold that they are not the only factor. The problem may be solved in this manner. We will include under the head of surroundings man's physical nature as determined by heredity, his material circumstances and surroundings, his social relations, and the stage of civilization into which he has been born. And then, recognizing the inherent creative and self-determining power of the human will, we are compelled to say that, while they are mighty formative influences, they control action only as the agent allows them to; that he is competent to utilize them to the furthering of his own ends, and that it is possible for him to be a peculiar man in the midst of most untoward surroundings. Giving all the credit one may desire to environment as a force in the development and direction of moral life, we must still remember that the environment is surroundings *plus* the man, and that the moral element is not in conditions but in choices.

But does not the Spencerian view of the unity of the race, or the doctrine of "social tissue" proposed by Mr. Leslie Stephen, militate against this theory of the moral ideal? The idea is individual; it is in my mind; I try to follow it. My neighbor has another ideal, and he tries to follow it. And so we have a multitude of individual ends and ideals of common good, while the great fact of recent investigation is the unity of social and national progress. Racial and National Ideals

The reply to this objection must be brief, yet it may serve to bring out with tolerable clearness the existence and character of national ideals. On the negative side, "society" is simply the name we give to a collection of individuals in various relations. Apart from these individuals, that to which it refers has no existence. As the tree is composed of cells, so society consists in individuals; and given the fact of racial unity, there is no necessary incompatibility between it and the possession of individual ideals. And, on the other hand, there are several considerations which indicate a positive harmony; *viz.*, the fact of mankind's common humanity, of the common human basis of the ideal, *i. e.*, self-consciousness, of the common surroundings of a nation or race which would shape the ends of conduct in a common way. And beyond these facts, are the conceptions, which go to the very roots of things, of the human self-consciousness as the reproduction under limitations of the Infinite Self-consciousness, and of the good as eternally realized in the Infinite Personality who is at once the Cause and the Goal of all our development. The expansion of this five-fold argument, and particularly of the last two ideas, would carry us far beyond our present limits. We can only say that they fully justify us in positing for the ideal an original "unity of design" — if we may so speak. And when, later, men become conscious of their ideals as such and seek to express them to their fellows, it is according to the reason which is inherent in any ideal, and which, appealing to the common self-consciousness, is adopted by it and so becomes an integral part of each individual ideal, that that ideal spreads and becomes the predominant active idea of a family, a city, or a nation. Thus we come to have a national ideal, a common ideal of action, shared in its general characteristics by the majority of citizens.

We should not confuse this with an individual ideal of a nation. What we ordinarily speak of in this way, is more properly an individual idea of a perfect nation. It is not an active idea, as is the moral ideal; its moral bearing is indirect. Only in so far as it is taken up into and changes personal ideals, and so secures certain individual actions, has it, as any other idea of common good, a moral effect.

Chapter II

INSTITUTIONS

An institution is literally something established. But searching behind this etymological statement, we find that institutions are set up, not only that they may stand, but that they may serve some purpose. What this their real nature is, we desire to learn, yet it is our wish just now to consider institutions only in themselves, as they appear. Looking at them, then, as they exist in the concrete, we find that they may be called organisms, for they seem to have, in a manner, a complete life within themselves. As is the case with other organisms, they are also centers of force. Each of them is the focus of a multitude of social fibers of afferent conduct and efferent influence. So far as their formation is concerned, they seem to be the deposits, in one realm of society and in another, of advancing civilization. Now one form of human activity and now another is affected by the progress, and in place of the old organism, there is deposited a changed, or an entirely new institution, whose office it is to conserve the advance which has been made, and the new order to which civilization has brought society. On the basis of these facts, we say, then, that institutions are, concretely, organisms, centers of force deposited by society, and conserving particular forms of social order.

<small>Definitions</small>

But this is not the only aspect in which institutions appear. As social action is made up of the conduct of individuals, so the institutions of society have no existence apart from the activity of those individuals. And given those individuals, institutions bear to them the relation of general forms under which their actions, which make up the action of society, take place. Together, the institutions form an orderly arrangement of human activity; they constitute the body, the *corpus* of social life. Hence, we obtain a second definition: Institutions are, in the abstract, habits of social living. And combining this and the previous one, we have the statement: Concretely, institutions are organisms, centers of force deposited by society, and conserving particular forms of social order. In the abstract, they are habits of social life.

Since institutions are, in one aspect, the forms under which human activity takes place, it follows that, in strictness, the concurrence of two persons in their action must found an institution; the action of a single individual, however, cannot, for institutions are social, they are habits of society. On the other hand, ordinarily the term "institution" is applied to the common mode of action of a large number of persons, or of the majority of the members of society.

As we examine institutions, we early inquire into their relation to other observed phenomena, perhaps with the ultimate aim of learning their sanction and cause. Beginning with the natural world, we find that institutions are in general agreement with the facts of physical nature, that certain types of institutions are found in the tropics, others mark the temperate zones, and still different forms exist in the more northerly regions. Likewise, there are certain peculiarities which generally distinguish the institutions of mountainous from those of level countries. We note also, that the attempt to transplant institutions is often a failure, and that it is only after certain conditions are complied with (*e. g.*, of education to the plane of a people living in different circumstances) that it can succeed. We, therefore, take general equilibrium with physical conditions as the first sanction of a social institution.

Sanctions and Causes of Institutions

The same thing must also be true as regards it connection with other institutions. All must be in equilibrium one with another, for they are severally members of one common civilization. In its advance, civilization has left one here and another there; the progress has most strongly affected now this institution and now that. But all together they form at any given stage the one coherent mass or order which we call society, and each institution must be in general equilibrium with the others, or else it cannot stand.

Another great sanction seems to be tradition. The customs of the fathers are a ground for many notions, and often their only ground. Not a few people look back with profound regret to the "good old times," and many men seem willing to act against their better judgment, in order that they may satisfy what they conceive to be the demands of *antiqui mores*.

Yet in the last analysis, from our present point of view, we find that the chief sanction of an institution is nothing else than its continued existence. This is *prima facie* evidence that it is in accord with the facts of nature, and proof of its equilibrium with the rest of the social order. However, such a statement is not entirely true. There are exceptions, for an institution which is the beginning of a new order may survive, although it is, to a certain extent, out of equilibrium with the rest of the organization; and by observation we are aware, that if it is firmly embedded, the influence which proceeds from it as a nucleus may result in a new society.

The existence of such exceptions suggests the question of the apparent causes of institutions. What is the cause in the equilibrium of institutions, these exceptions themselves tell us, *viz.*: the influence of a firmly embedded unadjusted institution. And this seems here to be the only cause. Looking for others, however, in the equilibrium with physical phenomena, it appears that the phenomena themselves are causes, and demand certain lines of action. The necessities of life compel hunting and agriculture, and likewise the fact of human gregariousness compels the institutions which, in general, we group under the family, society, and the state.

Examining institutions, then, from an external point of view, we observe as their sanctions, primarily, their continued existence, and secondarily, tradition and their adjustment in the physical and institutional equilibrium. And we note as their apparent causes the compelling forces of physical nature and the formative influences of existing institutions.

The thought of re-adjustment involves the idea of change and development in institutions, a deduction which observation verifies. Such movement is going on somewhere continually. In the language of equilibrium, there is a continuous re-adjustment. *Change in Institutions* The question arises whether it is progress. In some instances this seems to be the case, while in others, we think we notice regress. The fact is, that attention is drawn at one time to what is added, and at another to what is given up, and it is by what we observe that we pass judgment. In every instance there is, as history bears testimony, an absolute progress, though relatively it may seem to be retrogression. The form of this progress is a series of institutions, or, more properly, a series of variations in single institutions. Apparently, from time to time new institutions arise, but they are seen to be, in fact, only specializations of existing main divisions, the complexity which always accompanies higher forms of life. In order to verify this, we may run back over history in our thought, and the most cursory of examinations is sufficient to satisfy us that the real body of its events is the progress of institutions.

We now inquire more specifically as to the manner of their development. It sounds almost trivial to say that institutions change either slowly and imperceptibly, or suddenly. But we notice that a sudden development usually awakens in thoughtful minds anxiety as to its stability, while, regarding a slow evolution, there is no such solicitude. It is also observed that sudden changes do not always remain, while, on the other hand, a steady growth is in the main permanent. It would seem, then, that the real development of institutions, that which is stable and sure, is comparatively slow. We have further evidence of this from another quarter. Agitation is commonly the necessary forerunner of revolutionary changes. Yet in some cases, this agitation is a matter of years, while in others it is one of days. Now the object of agitation is to change or stimulate public opinion. This being true in all cases, we infer that when a long time is required, popular sentiment has to be changed practically from the start, while, in the second instance, it has been changing and only required stimulation. It seems, then, a legitimate conclusion from the character of the change in public opinion on which a revolution seems to depend, as well as from the anxiety which apparently sudden upheavals cause in thoughtful minds, that the real progress of institutions is gradual; and a tracing of the facts in any case will verify this induction.

In the next place, the growth of institutions brings increased number and complexity. This we have just noted as being really the specialization of primary institutions. It involves a deepening of their content and a more clear definition of what actions they endorse. It is also accompanied by a broadening of their range. The number of persons who act under certain forms is continually increasing. We notice, further, that all institutions do not develop together, or in equal ratio. Now one and now another is the center of movement, but the movement itself is general. Thus it is that we find a given age marked by certain prominent institutions, while in another others are most notable.

A part of the development of institutions seems to be their decay, just as in animal bodies that is a feature of life and change. Yet, as there, not the whole dies, but a part which is sloughed off. The new institution grows up beside the old, observed or unobserved. As it gathers strength, it takes the place of the old, either gradually or all at once, while at the same time the old is removed, either slowly by disintegration and absorption or quickly by an absolute destruction. It is some such process which is going on all the time, and by which the new is rising phœnix-like out of the old. There are, to be sure, forces which tend to the preservation of decadent institutions. A most potent one is tradition. Another is law. The one by the weight of its custom, and the other by its punishments, may for a long time continue old habits. Decaying, however, as they cease to be forms of common life, though they may in general cover certain fields of action, they cease in time to be accepted. And when society as a whole suffers from them, institutions are abolished. Yet they do not altogether die, for their influence is seen in the present. Their legacy is found in history and in literature. They serve as examples, persisting in more or less potent tradition. Nevertheless, what was their peculiar mark disappears; only the general, the social truth remains.

Having thus examined institutions, as they appear, we cast about for some scheme of classification. Temporarily, we find that we can divide them according to the stages of progress. We want, however, a classification of institutions in themselves. Range does not seem to offer a good criterion, for it calls only for differences in degree, and gives no distinct dividing lines. Content furnishes a better standard; and with its assistance we may classify institutions according to the fields of action which they cover. All social activity may thus

Classification of Institutions

be included in three divisions, according as it relates to the Subjugation of Material Nature, as it has to do with Social Organization, and as it promotes Individual Culture. We have then this classification :[1]

I — INSTITUTIONS RELATING TO THE SUBJUGATION OF NATURE.
    1. Material Progress.
    2. Ordinary Vocations.

II — INSTITUTIONS RELATING TO SOCIAL ORGANIZATION.
    1. The Family.
    2. The State.
    3. Religion.
    4. Social Customs.

III — INSTITUTIONS RELATING TO INDIVIDUAL CULTURE.
    1. Intellectual Education.
    2. Physical Culture.[2]

---

[1] Adapted from Mackenzie: Social Philosophy,

[2] 3. Spiritual Culture. These we have left untouched. Definition is difficult. In their more truly institutional form, they are closely related to Religion. But on the other hand, in their truest form they are confined to acts which are spiritual, private, and personal, of which autobiographies may give us hints, but as to which we really can have little knowledge.

CHAPTER III

STATIC RELATION OF IDEALS AND INSTITUTIONS—THEIR CORRESPONDENCE.

We have now considered ideals and institutions by themselves. We have defined the ideal as "an active idea of common good"; or, proximately, as the incarnation in idea of those principles of action which are considered morally ideal. *Introductory* An institution we have characterized as, concretely, an organism, a center of force deposited by society and conserving social order: and as, in the abstract, a habit of social living. In our discussion thus far, the attempt has been made to keep the ideal and the institution separate; but in the study of the ideal, frequent reference was made to society, and in that of institutions we alluded at least once to public sentiment. The fact is that the one cannot be thoroughly understood without reference to the other, and either of them, considered by itself, fails to disclose its true significance.

Institutions have been spoken of as forms of common activity, and such they are. But if we search below the surface of this statement, we lay bare a larger truth. Human action is for ends; it is prompted by desires whose satisfaction it seeks. This satisfaction is, as we have seen, the good, and the active idea of the common good is the moral ideal. Further, it is the ideal which, accepting the gratification of this or that desire as a means to its fulfilment, induces action, and it is the realization of the ideal at which we aim. Now action appears under the general forms of institutions; and so the two have a vital connection. Customs are, in a sense, the machinery of life. We may admire their delicacy or their stability, their plan and their beauty, but they have no vitality in themselves. As an ideal is not really such, is only an ordinary idea, unless we strive to realize it, so institutions of themselves are nothing. They serve humanity only as they are forms under and through which there is manifested the ideal. The facts of life are purposes and actions; ideals direct the first and institutions are the general 'forms for the second. And between the latter, as well as the former, there is an intimate connection. Yet, on the one hand, there are people who can content themselves with good intentions, as though the ideal had no real concern with life; and on the other, there are some who will only look on the phenomenal, that which appears, and who try to make moral conduct and physical action synonymous. Let us for a moment consider the ideal and the institution, each from the point of view of the other, that we may be the more certain of their real correspondence.

From the point of view of the ideal, institutions are general forms for its self-expression. They are its em-
Institutions from the Point of View of the Ideal bodiment, "the form and body of reason," objective morality. History, which is the record of past institutions, is recognized as also "the palæontology of moral ideals." Our definition of institutions as habits of social life is supported by this view. For a habit implies the consent, open or tacit, of those whose habit it is. So, too, our common surroundings are not sufficient to account for likeness of habit; but the oneness of human nature is. And that nature we call human, because it is self-conscious; and its moral characteristic as such is a common moral ideal. Again, from this point of view, institutions are simply forms of necessary life. Life is social, and as men are alike, this means that there must be established ways of action, *i. e.*, customs, institutions. They are necessary for the completion of the ideal. And it follows that, if the ideals of two groups of individuals are the same, their institutions will be the same, so far as circumstances allow.

But the question arises whether, as a matter of fact, all institutions have this connection with the ideal. It seems as though they did not; more especially as there are some in which, if we may so speak, less morality is required than in others. We may say first, however, that physical circumstances are not competent fully to account for any institution. They are simply the mould, or, to be more exact, the material of the mould, in which the manifestation of the ideal is cast. Now it often occurs, in the moulding process, that this mould is distorted from its original shape and changed in form. And in such an instance, we must of necessity refer to the action of the ideal that which cannot be accounted for by environment, for these are the two factors. But there are some actions which are mechanical. Habitually performed, they have become automatic. These, in their ultimate analysis, are by origin moral. Once they occupied our attention as they do not now; and if we doubt their real nature, we may test it by interfering with them. Yet it is to be remembered that only a small range of our activity ever becomes automatic. Gradually such a change takes place in the feeding of the engine and the oiling of the machinery, but not in the directing of the power. And the life of man is a field in which he must exercise all his faculties in the directing of his vital energy, if he would accomplish his greatest satisfaction.

Another question is whether institutions are the ideal's only manifestation. It seems to us that they are. Other forms in which the ideal appears are literature and philosophy. The first tells what has been lived in action and emotion. The latter is able to state the ideal quite accurately, because so largely untrammeled in its exercise. But both are expressions of moral ideas, rather than manifestations of the moral ideal. The relations of the ideal are solely with action.

Changing now our position, and looking at the ideal from the point of view of the institution, we note, first, that human actions, as carried on under the forms of institutions, are for ends; and as for ends, they are animated by purposes. We *The Ideal from the Point of View of the Institution* find that people do not act aimlessly under institutions. When we ask why they do a certain thing, they always have some reason ready. And without reference to the nature of the reply, the fact of a reason at all proves our assertion that the action is not unintentional. But further, the reason given is either the satisfaction of desire —" Because I want something " or " Because I think it will be to my advantage," or what is ultimately the same thing, obedience to a certain principle — " Because I ought to " or " Because other people do." Both these we recognize as expressions of what we have called the ideal. And so, by common account, ideals are at the basis of institutions.

Next we observe that men act *en masse* under certain institutions. This seems to involve a common idea of good. And not only do many individuals unite in action under these forms, but they act, under some of them at any rate, directly for the general welfare. These forms, then, involve some idea of common good which is shared by a number of individuals. We note also that variations in institutions are ordinarily referred to changes in public sentiment, the general opinion of what ought to be. Thus progress in institutions, as well as the existence of the institutions themselves, is commonly laid at the door of the moral ideal. From the standpoint of institutions, therefore, the ideal is a generally shared idea of common good, for which institutions are the ordinary modes of manifestation, and which, by its activity, produces change in them.

The division between institutions and the ideal thus grows more and more unreal. We may separate the musician and the organ, but then the organ is only wood and metal, and of the organist no one is aware. Together they constitute the whole. So with the ideal and institutions, except that the relation is more vital. Sever them from the ideal, and the institutions may possibly remain for a little, but they are only inert forms; neither is the ideal manifested. The two go hand in hand, they have an inherent connection, they answer the one to the other. The ideal involves the institution, and the institution involves the ideal.

Institutions' and the Ideal Constitute one Whole

But some facts are lying in wait for us. Individual action, it is observed, does not always accord with established institutions, and it is common testimony that customary action does not always agree with the demands of the ideal. For instance, the reformer does what he thinks he ought, what the ideal commands him to do, when it is contrary to the institutions of society; and, in similar manner, the criminal does what he desires, in the face of social disapproval.

Objections Considered

To explain these cases, we must remember that institutions are primarily and only social. They posit for their existence a number of people. On the contrary, the ideal, while having regard to persons as in social relations, is first individual. So it may command actions which have no allotted place in existing institutions, or are even opposed to them. To be sure, when two persons agree in matters of conduct, it is, as we have said, theoretically the foundation of a new custom. But ordinarily, both institutions and ideals (as social and national) refer to bodies of citizens. This, then, being the situation, it is a fact that institutions and ideals do not and cannot exactly correspond. And we would not desire to prove it otherwise, if we could. For entire correspondence would mean that the ideal was fully realized, or to put it in more startling form, that the existing condition of things was ideal. What we do maintain is that the institutions of society correspond with the general moral ideal; that, for the majority of the citizens, institutions and ideals in a broad way answer to each other.

But once again, the question may be asked, Do not institutions exist without ideals? Two cases may be cited in support of this. A king may impose an institution upon his subjects. An institution may be continued by tradition, when no ideal answers to it. As to the second instance, we doubt the existence of any such state of things. More likely the questioner misinterprets the facts; knowing that the custom is traditional, he assumes that it is supported by no ideal. It may, however, be true that the ideal has passed a good ways beyond established customs, some cause or other having hindered their development. The society, then, is preparing for new institutions, and the old will ultimately be assimilated, or destroyed. Yet the present order has some likeness to the common ideal, or it could not still exist. The absurdity of a custom which absolutely no one favored, on any account, is apparent on the surface. The first case, however, is from real life — sovereigns do impose upon their peoples customs which are burdens grievous to be borne. Yet, in every case, according as the custom either remains or falls into disuse, slowly or at once, it is either accepted or rejected by the people. They may accept the institution in itself; or they may allow it to continue, in accord with their ideal of obedience to the king. But in both cases they accept it. And if it is removed, it is because the people quietly refuse to act under it, because the ruler sees that they are becoming uneasy under it, or by means of a revolution — in each instance because it is not in agreement with the ideal of the nation.

We hold, then, by our former conclusion, and say that, in general, it is true that the institutions of a given society and the moral ideal of the majority of its people are in correspondence, the former with the latter.

Chapter IV

THE PARALLEL DEVELOPMENT OF IDEALS AND INSTITUTIONS

Proofs and Objections

Ideals exist and develop. Institutions also exist, and they too, as we say, develop. At any given stage of the development, as we have just seen, the ideal and the institution in a general way correspond. It is, then, but the shortest step, the most direct deduction, by which we arrive at the parallel progress of ideals and institutions in historical development. But our consideration, thus far, has only established their correspondence in organic periods of civilization, in the nodes, so to speak, of social development, and not in the internodes. The question therefore arises whether, in all the steps of the evolution, the ideal and the institution are parallel.

We have admitted that they never correspond exactly, since, if they did, such a condition would involve stagnation. More than this, institutions can never be an adequate manifestation of the existing ideal. The fact of surrounding circumstances necessitates certain restrictions, even though the situation may be somewhat changed and adapted. And the most accurate expression which we can give the ideal, we confess, is that in which philosophy presents it. Yet this does not do away with any parallelism or connection between institution and ideal. Inasmuch as we have arrived at their correspondence, we know that they are capable of inter-relation in thought, and that, therefore, they must have a logical relation in reality. The "logic of events" and the growth of the ideal are one.

A fruitful source of error in this matter, and one which we must bear in mind, is that what we would naturally view as the most important characteristic of the ideal may not really predominate. For instance, in an extreme case, a civilization is completely destroyed by an invading army; the conqueror imposes new institutions and new customs. And what then becomes of our parallelism? We reply that the fact of conquest has produced as great a change in ideals as in institutions, or one of the same kind. The dominant characteristic of the ideal is now obedience; the one habit of life, in which, for the time being, all particular institutions are included, is servitude. The ideal demands submission to the will of the conqueror as the only good action, for simple existence becomes the end, and only thus can it be attained.

And this submission must continue either without end, or till such time as resistance can successfully be made. And it is so in every case. Men act under institutions for ends. When they cease to act for their desired ends under given institutions, those institutions crumble. But activity continues; and the institutions which are really such are always those forms under which activity, as a matter of fact, takes place.

There is another matter here which demands attention. It presents itself in the form of a question, Is development always progress? And it is emphasized by the query, How can it be, when we see civilizations completely destroyed, and whole nations sink lower and lower in degradation? To begin with the individual, we recognize that there is some change, however slight, in the ideal each day. One's actions, too, vary somewhat from day to day. From these facts it follows that a person will be to-morrow better or worse, and that permanently, than he is to-day. In society, institutions, as in a sense crystallizations, do not steadily change; but we know that popular sentiment, on which they depend, is all the time changing little by little. Though these changes seem slight and comparatively unimportant, we must not overlook them, for they are making up from day to day the sum-total of development.

Development is Always Progress

But progress ordinarily suggests to our minds an upward movement, an advance, along certain preconceived lines. We mistake in so limiting progress, and in designating all else as retrogression. Mere retrogression is only a theoretical possibility. And even then, it is really an impossibility, for were there no other difference, there would be, first, that of time, and second, that numerical difference which must necessarily exist between two things in all other respects exactly the same. Any development is progress; it involves new content, and therefore must be progress. The question from the ethical point of view is not, Is this progress? but, In what direction is this progress? "Whereunto shall these things grow?"

Direction of Progress
And so our last question now is as to the general direction of progress. As we think back, the most natural designation of historical development is under the three adjectives, material, intellectual, and moral. But these make an outward rather than a real division. They are phases of action, not fundamental lines of the growth of conduct. In both institutions and ideals we have previously noted a common manner of development, *viz.*, broadening of range and deepening of content; and these are the two lines of what we call, collectively, historical development. We may, perhaps, make them more tangible under the titles of increased intelligence, answering to content, and broader sympathy, which is the correlate of wider range. Content and range indicate the directions, and deepening and broadening the manner of progress. In another way of putting it, the center of all development is personality. As broadening in range, it includes more and more individuals as complete persons; as deepening in content, it reveals new depths and resources of self-conscious individuality.

Having thus developed the theory of the historical parallelism of ideals and institutions, it is our purpose to trace that development in history. But we defer this for a little, in order that we may first make our exposition analytically complete. The following chapter, then, presents the logical outcome of what has preceded, rather than the central point of the thesis' contention.

CHAPTER V

DYNAMIC RELATION OF IDEALS AND INSTITUTIONS — PRIORITY AND CAUSALITY OF IDEALS

In previous chapters, it may have seemed as though our exposition involved an intentionally hidden element, and that it was rather under the restraint of a predetermined logical analysis. But now that we have come substantially to its end, there is no longer any call for reservation. A complete statement would be: Not only has there been, historically, a parallel development of ideals and institutions, but in that parallel development, the ideal has been prior to, and causally connected with, its corresponding institutions.   *Introductory*

Already in treating of the Correspondence of Ideals and Institutions, we have allowed that, in many individuals, the ideal is in advance of existing institutions. This would seem to lend color to the first part of the statement, to make its truth not only possible, but probable. We may briefly support the two assertions.

I. The ideal precedes its corresponding institutions. There are two things which can precede new institutions, environment and men, and both of these must precede them. For if environment be left out, men have nothing on or by which to act; and if men be omitted only environment remains without agents. Both are necessary conditions of the existence of institutions. If, now, we analyze these two factors, in the first, we find environment consisting of physical nature and a preceding state of society, *i. e.*, precedent institutions; in the second factor, men have, roughly speaking, three characteristics : physically, they live, intellectually, they think, morally, they act for the satisfaction of desires, that is, the manifestation of ideals, as we have already seen. None of these five factors can be omitted, and, by hypothesis, they are all precedent to the new institutions, as included under the exhaustive division into men and   *Priority* facts. Therefore ideals precede their corresponding institutions.[1]

Aside, however, from this analytic proof, we have the evidence of the nature of ideals and institutions, and the direct reasoning from them. For the distinguishing characteristic of the ideal is that it guides conduct. It is an active idea. This it is which gives it its preëminence over the other ideas of common good. As such an active idea, the ideal must therefore precede, not only the conduct itself, but the institutions as well, for they are the forms under which conduct occurs, the habits of social living, according to which human activity takes place.

II. The ideal is causally connected with its corresponding institutions. Priority of the ideal being established, its causal connection with institutions is a possibility. In our analysis of the factors which precede institutions, we found all five necessarily coming before the institution in point of time. Now temporal relation is only a contingent, not a necessary form of an existing connection. The necessary relation is logical. So all the factors will be in some measure causally connected with institutions, and at the same time we cannot speak of any one as *the* cause.

Causality

But they may be causes in varying degrees. First, distinguishing active from inactive, we mark man as the agent, while environment and precedent institutions act as conditioning causes. Now, in man the three factors make up one whole; yet they are not on an equality. The intellectual is higher than the physical, and the ultimate end of all life, both physical and intellectual, is character, that is, that which is moral. Physical life is essential to human activity. Ideas are our reasonable apprehensions of things. But in matters of conduct, it is accepted ideas of ends which the ideal takes up into itself, and whose realization it commands. This is the *rationale* of human

---

[1] For the benefit of the technical reader, it may be said that reference is here made to institutions as social phenomena. It may be held that, in their primary and fundamental definition, ideals and institutions are practically synonymous; as an ideal is not an ideal except as its fulfilment is the end of the agent's action, and institutions are the habitual modes of the action — which at bottom is the volition — of a number of similar agents. But the definition of an institution, as in this psychological sense a habit, is, in strictness, one which could not be made at the outset, but rather after such consideration as leads to the understanding of its relation to the ideal. We have, in general, referred to institutions as they appear, apart from this special signification. Of the institution, as in this psychological sense a habit, the temporal priority of the ideal would not be true, for the ideal and the institution would have simultaneous existence. The causality of the ideal, however, would remain the same, for the logical relation between ideals and institutions is necessary and universal.

action in the individual. And it is very apparent that it is the ideal which is the vital cause of conduct. Now, what is true of one man as man, is true of all. Simply the common habits of life are what we call institutions. And these habits are common, conditions being similar, as a common ideal commands the activity which they formulate. Ideals are, then, the causes of institutions; and in the ultimate analysis, the relation is one of final causality.

There are those who do not accept this view of the Causality of Ideals. To this number belong, for instance, many socialists and communists, if we may judge from their programs. They expect to elevate men by improving their surroundings and the conditions of their lives. The same is true of many philanthropists. On the other hand, the secret of such enterprises as Hull House, Chicago, and Andover House, Boston, of the social work of General Booth "In Darkest England," and of all sorts of missionary endeavor, is the changing of men's moral and social conditions by the prior elevation of their ideals. Not upon doing for men, but upon the possibility of persuading them to do for themselves, rests the assurance of ultimate success in the endeavor to elevate mankind.

Part II

HISTORICAL

Chapter I

THE PARALLEL DEVELOPMENT OF GREEK IDEALS AND INSTITUTIONS

We commence our historical investigation with the Greeks, as the earliest people, well known to us, who have left a definite and permanent impression upon history. We begin with the first organic stage of society of which we have a description, that pictured in the Greek epic. And we shall expect to find in the four stages of Greek society — the Homeric, the Transitional, the Attic, and the Hellenic — first of all a development of the moral ideal.[1]

Preliminary

I — DEVELOPMENT OF THE IDEAL

The ideal man of the first period is presented in the Iliad and Odyssey. Naturally, we do not find all his characteristics given in tabulated form, nor do we find any of the heroes embodying them all. We are able, however, to gather from these poems that the ideal of the Homeric times was the victorious warrior,

Homeric Ideal

> "Of ready wit and dauntless courage, proved
> In every danger; and to Pallas dear."

He was strong physically, like Menelaus of "broad chest and brawny arm," and like Agamemnon, "king of men," heroic both in bearing, which comes from his noble lineage, and in action, which springs from a warlike heart. He made great boast of his abilities and of his reputation, but all qualities he valued chiefly according to the results which they brought, and when he stripped the spoil of battle from his fallen enemy, he considered that he gained one of the great good things of life.

---

[1] It may be well to make note of the fact that Professor Mahaffy, in his "Social Life in Greece," maintains "the sameness of Greek character and social ideas through all periods of Greek literature;" and he states as the common maxim of all Greek life, "Work for youth, counsel for maturity, and prayers for old age." (Fragment from Hesiod; Maxim given by Chiron to Achilles; preserved by Harpocration from an oration by Hyperides. *Davies, J.:* Hesiod and Theognis.) While other writers make few statements either way, there seems to be the tacit acceptance of a progress in morality, as well as in knowledge and art. And if Professor Mahaffy is correct in his general statement, he must at least allow a very wide and somewhat differing interpretation of these rules, in the various stages we are about to study.

He did not, however, despise labor. In times of peace, he busied himself in the supervision of his estate, and found recreation in the pleasures of his home, in feasting and conversation with guest-friends, and in music and manly sports. His chief dignity was that which he had as the member of a family or tribe. To its maintenance and defence he would bend all his energies in time of need, and equally, in time of peace, he had its welfare very much at heart. As a member of the family he was closely connected with the household divinities, and if he was its head, he was also its high priest; in any case, he would reverence the gods and obey them. Thus, he was, first, a warrior, yet not a despiser of toil. He was fond of social pleasures, yet not a glutton. He was deeply imbued with piety, at once filial and religious. He may have been rude, but he was not coarse.

We notice, possibly first of all, that this ideal is almost entirely external. The ideal man is the perfection of the physical nature. And to so great an extent is this true, that one might perhaps be led to deny what we call morality to those who manifested this ideal. Their nearest approach to it is in obedience to the gods, and this is largely a means to the maintenance of their personal honor and that of the tribe. It is determined, not by a sense of obligation, but by personal attachment to the gods, and by fear of their hatred and ill-will. The highest services and the greatest enjoyments occupy the physical man. Life has to do almost entirely with external phenomena, and is "according to nature." So far as man speculates, it is concerning the relations of things around him; and his thinking is without system. His life is all in terms of his environment. In keeping with this ideal is the primary meaning of the word ἀρετή, which we translate "excellence." Derived from the name *Ares* (Lat. *Mars*), its first application is to the fight. This is its Homeric significance, physical excellence shown by bravery in the fight; and the ideal man, a Greek by birth, is himself a hero, and is devoted to the gods and to his family.

Ideal External

Since the ideal is physical the great power is brute force. He who cannot protect himself, finds, as a rule, no protection from his fellows. The weak is the unsuccessful type; the ideal demands strength; force is the masculine quality. The great demand is for personal prowess and the gaining of the victory. Goodness or conscientiousness, so far as it was exhibited, was thought, on the whole, to be weakness. To be sure, truthfulness was recognized as praiseworthy, but there was constant recourse to the deception which was never known to fail. Similarly, the average of Greek courage was, some think, not very high, but the spur which was competent to rouse it all was its utility to the gaining of the victory.[1]

There are facts which lead us to believe that this ideal is the ideal of what we may call the court. Somewhat opposed to it is that presented in the Hesiodic poems. Here the ideal man lives a life of simplicity. He occupies himself with the care of his farm and his flocks and herds. With him, the divinities are the patrons of morality; they are the Fates, who set the bounds of mortal life, and the god Hermes, upon whose images, in the later days, moral precepts were engraved. In general, the ideal life is frugal and moral. Some are of the opinion that the works of Hesiod are a polemic against the society represented in the Homeric epic. But — and we might expect it from them as being two extremes — in essential characteristics the two are similar. The main difference is in the points on which the poet throws emphasis, and in the occupations to which the different men are largely confined. Both are external, and have to do with the physical man, and in a certain way the ideal is, as we say to-day, "practical."

Hesiodic Ideal

We find the two pictures united in the life of the city-state. The place of the former unconsciousness was here being taken, gradually and with increasing rapidity, by intelligent action; or, more correctly, where there had been almost nothing, there was now beginning to be the consciousness of personality and of human freedom. In the early period, the bravery of the heroes in battle, and the cowardice which they sometimes displayed, had been laid to the presence or absence in them of

Ideal of Transitional Period — In Life of City-State

---

[1] It ought, perhaps, to be said, that we do not mean that the men of the Homerid deliberately set this picture of life before themselves, and tried to realize it in what they did. Certainly they did not in the way in which we should do the same thing. It would be a great mistake to clothe them with our powers of introspection. They more likely acted as a child does to-day, largely as they had been taught, and from the incentive of current events, for external and apparent ends. It is embedded in their action, that we find the ideal which we have been describing, unconscious but active.

some god, and the strength which he would impart. Now men began to speak of these as personal qualifications, and to take the credit for noble action to themselves. The same externality still marked the ideal. Although, more and more, man was thought of as intellectual as well as physical, for some time the good was to be attained as against others, rather than in one's self; and this was so, whether we make our point of view the individual or the state. Instead, however, of the victory in war which the early ideal had demanded, it was victory in any contest that was now required. And though the ideal man was still a warrior on occasion, his primary object in battle was not personal glory, but the defence of the state. Indeed, to so large a degree was his life "political," that in the success of the state he himself succeeded, and in its failure he felt that he too would utterly fall. Along with this patriotic devotion, there was sometimes present a mercenary, self-seeking spirit. But, in general, this was the ideal of the middle Greeks: a warrior-citizen, emphatically a Greek, and a citizen of some city; a member, likewise, of a family, preferably noble.¹ As a warrior-citizen, his chief relations were religious and political, those of religion remaining from the preceding period, and political feelings, now the strongest bonds of his life, being the new growth. Citizenship brought to him certain rights and protections, but there were also incident upon him certain obligations which he must fulfil; and all his acts, as those of every citizen, were looked on as first affecting the internal welfare of the State.

In Oracular Responses

It is at about this time that we find the oracles most reverenced and trusted by the Greeks. And since they were under the control of a prudent priesthood, they should furnish us a fair index of the best of current opinions and beliefs. The greater part of their deliverances have disappeared, especially those relating to moral principles and to questions of conduct, but from the scattered utterances which remain we get a few hints as to the prevailing moral ideal. The oracle of Apollo at Delphi refused to answer one who came to it, having left his comrade in danger of death; no one could consult it against the interests of the Hellenes; it foretold woes for the perjurer, and

---

¹ This, of course, as a matter which could not be governed, in strictness was not included, but rather the honor and nobility that followed from it.

censured men and cities for their vanity; and to the question, Who is the happiest man? it gave answer, "Phaidios, who died for his country."

But soon — early in the age of Pericles — there was a noticeable change in the character of thought. Really the result or out-cropping of long development, it seems as though the Greeks had suddenly become conscious of themselves. *Attic Ideal* There was a strong infusion of learning and of knowledge of current events into the nature of the ideal. And whereas the ideal had tied one up to the interests of the state, to the exclusion of much of personal welfare, it now called more and more for the man of individual culture. This is really a radical change in the character of the ideal. In the early times, it had held aloft the unthinking, unintrospective, physical man, busied with external things; in the middle period there had been a gradual working over and modification, the general characteristics remaining much the same. But in this later time, there was a marked coming to consciousness of the possibilities of man's nature. The chief bond of union became law, and was no longer personal attachment as among the heroes. The ideal man was as well an individual, as a member of the city-state. The manifestation of excellence was both in the stability and glory of the state, and in the perfection of the personalities of its citizens. From this type the external was not excluded; indeed, it was cultivated. But perfection also included the internal, and this, in increasing measure, was recognized as the real self.

This ideal, however, bore in its flower the seeds of its degeneration. While the hold of the state upon its citizens was yet strong, the uppermost questions soon ceased to be, Is it to the advantage *Hellenic Ideal* of the state? Instead, there was no blame attaching to any conduct, provided it did not openly menace the welfare of the state. With the greater number, the idea of personality referred to capacities for personal gratification, and involved license. The side of individuality which they discovered was that which dictates freedom from physical labor. And so there arose the typical expression of the changed ideal, the Athenian gentleman — he whose political apathy Demosthenes in vain attempted to dispel. The object of life was not the conquest of the enemies of the state; and so far as the desire for victory was active, it found its satisfaction in "eristic prize-fighting." The main object of existence was the elegant employment of leisure.

The theories of the great trio of philosophers, though on a higher plane, are in many respects typical of life in the Age of Pericles. They inculcate, to a large degree, an ideal of all-round manhood. But the development of the latent tendencies which produced the Hellenic ideal is apparent in the Stoic and Epicurean off-shoots, and in the decided preponderance of the latter in the matter of popular following. While evidently lacking in strength, the ideal of this last period demanded a civilized refinement and an intellectual culture that were beyond all which had preceded.

II — PARALLEL DEVELOPMENT OF INSTITUTIONS RELATING TO THE SUBJUGATION OF NATURE

Parallel with this progress of the ideal, there was a progress of institutions. We find, for instance, the difference very plainly marked between the Homeric times and those of Pericles, and in the middle period, in a number of instances, we are able to note the advance.

We naturally find a considerable difference in the common occupations. In early Greece, since the ideal man was the great warrior and the owner of broad acres, the only worthy pursuits were arms and agriculture. In the middle period, when the population massed itself in cities and life put on the city aspect, men were occupied with the affairs of the state, and its commands and welfare received their whole attention. Yet some found time to make money, and even to so great an extent was this true that Theognis laments, "The mass of men know but one virtue — to be rich." Though this was the view of one who was considerable of a pessimist in his own day, the words were nevertheless prophetic. In later Athens, the sense of personality, newly acquired, prompted to the seeking of individual gain and personal pleasure, first, as citizens of the state, and then, at the expense of the state's well-being. Many of the poorer citizens received their support at the public expense as dicasts, and the largesses which were made by Pericles were but a concession to the growth of the same influence. Plato says that Pericles made the people "lazy, frivolous, and sensual";

but this was his polemic in the rôle of a reformer. What he attacked was really the development of hitherto latent germs. The gentleman of Athens of the later days was bent on the elegant use of his leisure, and it was in pursuit of this that he whiled away his hours in the *agora* or at the bath, mingling in the common talk or hanging on the lips of some popular teacher, always eager to hear or tell some new thing.

It is, then, not very amazing that for him, more than for his ancestors, all the trades and handicrafts were on a low level. Most honor was accorded the architect, for he ministered to the religious and citizen spirit, as well as to the æsthetic sense of beauty. But sculptors and painters were looked on as only makers of statues and makers of pictures, as others made arms and implements. And yet it is during this period that we see in and about Athens those magnificent temples and that multiplicity of statues spring into being. From the Homeric times there had been a marked increase in comfort, and the rude splendor of the early days had given way to a stately beauty which is still the wonder of the world. Yet beyond this there developed only general luxuriousness, and a search for that which is merely beautiful.

	CAUSALITY.	MATERIAL WELFARE
1	Rude splendor,	Corresponds to demands of external, physical ideal.
2	Growing comfort,	Due to demands of increasingly intellectual ideal, also calling for victory.
3	Greater magnificence,	Due to ideal of individual culture in the state.
4	Luxuriousness,	Due to ideal of personal gratification.

	COMMON OCCUPATIONS	
1	Warrior and farmer, arms and agriculture,	Corresponds to physical (and family) ideal.
2	City affairs,	Due to political ideal.
3	(Also 2) Getting rich,	Due to utilitarian tinge of ideal, good as victory; and to ideal of individual culture.
4	Individual gain, pleasure, support at public expense,	Due to ideal of personal gratification.
	Use of leisure,	Due to ideal of Athenian gentleman.
	Artisans looked down upon.	Due to the same.

III — PARALLEL DEVELOPMENT OF INSTITUTIONS RELATING TO SOCIAL ORGANIZATION

But these might be considered rather as phenomena of the change in Greek national life, than as an integral part of it. We find the development *par excellence* in the institutions of society which we more commonly call by that name — the family, the state, religion, and social customs.

The Family — In the early days, the family was a religious institution, its members being bound together in the worship of departed ancestors. The life was in general one of purity. Each man, the chiefs being excepted, was the husband of one wife. Society was as yet unartificial, and woman was nearly on an equality with man, his help-meet. She ate with him at table, she was a sharer of his life when he was not at war. To her was given over the care and direction of the home. But with the change to city life, there was a change in the position of woman. She was secluded, according to the Asiatic custom. While greater laxity was allowed to the husband, on the contrary, the strictest fidelity was exacted from the wife, and if, with or without reason, he put her away, it was she that must bear the reproach and not he. At the first, the marriage tie had been rather one of custom, its chief safeguard being the family's position as the main organization of society. But now, as we shall more plainly see in the consideration of the state, the primary bond changed to one of citizenship. The tie of patriotism and friendship became stronger than that of the family, and to meet the opportunity thus afforded, there was a growing tendency away from purity of life. Toward the close of the period, woman was little more than a domestic slave; and in the next, we find Aristotle saying that the intellectual capacity of women is different from that of men (thus explaining the current idea that women should not be expected to know anything). For the men of his day, Demosthenes declared, "We have *hetairae* to please us, and wives to bear us children and to care for our households." Evidently the wife had lost her old position as the companion of her husband. Marriage, which was at first acknowledged by a public ceremony, had been gradually stripped of its formalities, and reduced to that which was but its original essence. Never a civil or religious act, though religious forms had accompanied its recognition, it was primarily simply the living together as man and wife. And it now became only a domestic relationship, and the tie could be made or broken without great ado.

There are some who declare that the Spartan matron was the Greek ideal woman of these, and, in fact, of all times, or that Andromache, for instance, and Antigone are the types of the womanly ideal; but to us the facts seem otherwise. These characters may have been and doubtless were admired, but they were not the ideal of action. In the later days, the wife had greater credit than formerly in this, that whereas heredity had been regarded as existing only through the father, Aristotle declared that children were equally the offspring of father and mother. But in only one thing did the old position of the wife remain, she had the care of the children.

Was the Spartan the ideal woman?

	CAUSALITY.	THE FAMILY
1	Homeric family,	Corresponds to place of family in ideal and to lack of coarseness. Characteristics of ideal as external, physical and utilitarian show possibilities of evil development, when men became self-conscious, unless something be added.
2	Loss of regard for family,	Due to growth of political ideal. Tendency to make family only a means to increase the state; so to degrade it.
3	Increase of the same,	Due to same and to selfish ideal of individual culture.
4	Greater degradation,	Due to ideal of self-gratification.
	Glossing over,	Due to ideal of elegance and luxury.
	Some betterment in family life,	Due to presence of some control in the ideal.

In political institutions we find a very marked development. The early state was a patriarchal kingdom. Its basis was religious. The chieftain was such by virtue of his position as high-priest of the tribe.

The State — Early Period

The mass of the people constituted a general assembly which met to hear the results of the sittings of the king's council of nobles. But while they were allowed to express dissent from the plans which had been adopted, they could not change them. The king, however, was not a sovereign with power over the people, although his kingship was hereditary by primogeniture; he was only the leader in battle and the chief executive. The unit of the kingdom was the deme, a community having a leader of its own, and represented by him, as a member of the king's council, in the deliberations of the nation. Among the members of the deme there was acknowledged mutual responsibility. If a member did wrong to any one outside, all were guilty, and if one was harmed, all were to take revenge. Thus in the deme, each individual was a unit, but in the kingdom the unit was a single community. The chief was the king, not of the people, but of the demes.

<small>Transitional</small>

The middle period commences with the death of King Codrus in battle, and the change from kings to elected archons. Afterward there was a further change to archons for ten years, and finally to nine archons for one year. The general government was in reality at one time a tyranny and at another an oligarchy; all through it was aristocratic. The family gradually lost its political significance. The city, which was formerly cantonal, became municipal, and its internal government was developed. In the time of Solon, the pressure of the resident aliens and the peasants (becoming conscious of themselves as men) upon the old Eupatrids compelled the new constitution, and the establishment under Cleisthenes of a pure democracy. This reached its highest development in the Age of Pericles, when each man consciously used his citizenship for the welfare of the state, and everyone was jealous of Athenian honor. Parallel to this increase of the popular power was the gradual curtailment of that of the Areopagus. Deprived, one by one, of its privileges, the tablets containing the laws were in Cleisthenes' time brought down from Mars' Hill to the market place, and the weighty body of ancient and honorable nobility was allowed to nurse its dignity in stately elegance. The last step in the transformation was taken under the leadership of Aristides the Just. The essential qualification of wealth for office-holding was removed, and whereas, at first, nobility of birth had been necessary, now all classes of citizens, irrespective of wealth or lineage, were alike eligible.

<small>Attic</small>

In this state, the Athenians had full liberty; and in that liberty were comprised personal safety, freedom of speech, the right of intermarriage with all families, and the right of holding property. That this change was slow in coming about goes almost without the saying — and, indeed, we have tacitly implied it. Both the Eupatrids and the men of the mountain and of the shore hated each the tyranny of the other. Among the Eupatrids, each youth took the memorable oath which Aristotle has preserved, " I will be at enmity with the *demos*, and will do it all the harm I can." But the growth of the new ideal brought about, in the end, the new constitution and the new adjustment of society. In a sense, however, the democracy was a tyranny. The Greeks were by nature aristocrats ; the range of the ideal included only Greeks. Hence, in the outlying provinces, the inhabitants had no voice in the management of their affairs, and in the city it was true before many years that aliens paid the taxes and slaves did the work, together supporting the state, while it was conducted by its citizens. The democracy was a tyranny, too, in that, in the hands of the populace, the government became a machine turned against the noble and wealthy.

To maintain the democracy in the height of its power was a thing most difficult ; in fact, it was beyond the ability (or stability) of the Greeks. In the ideal of personal freedom, only a few were aware of the accompanying necessity of self-control, and so, for the crowd, freedom, which soon meant license, made democracy mean anarchy. Interest in personal attainment and in pleasure took precedence of the call of the state. No longer did the citizens care to go to war. The theater and the baths, the conversation of the market and the pettifogging of the assembly were more to their taste. Government became a sort of instrument, manipulated for private ends, and the public revenue was spent in catering to the whims of the people. The existing corruption appears, for instance, in the open trade of writing speeches, whereas cases had formerly been decided simply on the evidence, and men had appeared for themselves, and in the scramble for offices to which there attached no salary — but countless bribes. Rulers prided themselves, not on the purity of their administrations, but on the degree in which the public praised their benefactions. It is this which causes Mahaffy to say that the democracy was a failure. It had, in truth, fallen among thieves, but through them there was worked out, nevertheless, the changed ideal of manhood. And the old Greek families as truly exhibit it, for they drew away from public

<small>Hellenic</small>

affairs to the privacy of their homes; and some of them in treason, perhaps to carry out their oath, went over to the side of Sparta in the struggles between the two states. It is possible, and undoubtedly correct, to see in this a preparation for what is called Hellenism; but it should be noted that that, as this, came about through the spread and change of the moral ideal.

Neither the splendor of the Age of Pericles nor the gross corruption about 430 B. C. seems to represent the real condition of affairs and the true development. The last was in a way the result of the first; very much as to-day we see men, who have suddenly come to wealth, live in elegance and retain their good sense, while, in instances not a few, their children or grandchildren show a great degeneration. After both phases had passed, the political condition seems to have been really more stable than before. Of this resultant period, Grote is led to say, "there are no acts which attest so large a measure of virtue and judgment pervading the whole people as the proceedings after the Four Hundred and the Thirty."[1] This may be thought, perhaps, an over-estimate, but something tolerably near it might be construed from the progress of the ideal. Men had finally learned by hard experience that there was a large place for control in both political and individual freedom.

The whole development and the subsequent political ruin at Athens were foretold and earlier experienced by the Ionian colonies. In the first days of the Athenian state, the numerous alien and Greek-alien residents, as they could not become citizens, and were rather a growing menace to the city, were compelled, periodically, to emigrate and form colonies, distant from the mother state. These colonists were Greeks in all but name and blood, and their foster-mother's selfish, aristocratic tendencies, and the Greek ideal, appear in their history. By energetic activity, they soon built up a well-ordered government, and became the leaders of the surrounding peoples, keeping themselves, however, distinctly separate from them. Democracy was reached here about a century sooner than at Athens, since it was possible without hindrance to put into immediate action the ideal of the people at home. And when, at a later time, these cities refused to unite with one another, each holding to its own in-

<small>Similar Development in Ionia</small>

---

[1] Grote: History of Greece, viii: 176.

dividualism and superiority, they fell a prey to Lydia and to Persia in turn, long before the conquests of Philip and Alexander.

Among the Greeks at home, there were always some who saw the advantages of political unity, but to cause the majority to endorse any such project, there must be some immediate gain apparent. The first attempt at union was on a religious basis, the Amphictyonic League. Attempts at Greek Unity This for a long time held its own, because of its relation to the great festivals; but at no time was the bond very close, and the league, as a league of the states for confederacy in government, was practically of little significance. The only kind of political union which could survive the birth was, in the nature of the case, some sort of a supremacy. On this basis, there were established the successive hegemonies of Athens, of Sparta, of Thebes, and of Macedon. Only the last, however, was permanent, and it was a conquest. So long as each state was of sovereign power, it refused to become in any sense tributary, except under compulsion, and the influence of the ideal of individual aggrandizement made it the immediate foe of all its neighbors. Moreover, the common feeling of Greece sided with the state, which, having joined a league or been subjected to another state, attempted to free itself and to assert its own autonomy. In still later times, the broadening of the ideal allowed of the formation of the Achæan League with somewhat better success, for at length the people had many of them come to see the ideal citizen as submitting all his rights to the good of the community, and however imperfectly this was realized, it was much better understood than in the earlier days.

	CAUSALITY.	THE STATE
1	Homeric state,	Corresponds to place of family and of religious observances in the ideal.
	Community,	To ideal of all men as laboring.
	Natural government,	As the ideal is unconscious.
2	Loss of power of family,	Due to new political ideal.
	Oligarchy and tyranny,	Due to ideal to be realized against others, rather than in one's self.
	Class agitations,	Due to growing consciousness of personality.
3	Tyranny of people,	Due to surviving ideal.
	Democracy,	Due to ideal of personality.
	Liberty in state,	Due to same and ideal of self-culture.
4	Anarchy, corruption, and catering of rulers to crowd,	Due to ideal of personal gratification.
	Apathy and withdrawal of old families from politics (and to Sparta),	Due to same and to ideal of elegant employment of leisure.

	CAUSALITY.	GREEK CONFEDERACIES
1	Amphictyonic League,	Corresponds to place of religious observances in ideal.
2	Hegemonies,	Due to ideal of good as attained against others.
3		Development of ideal of individual culture preparing way for
4	Conquest,	Due to ideal of self-gratification and consequent apathy.
	Achæan League,	Due to faint presence in ideal of control as necessary to true freedom.

Next in the order of institutions stands religion. We find its customs occupying, in the earlier days, a much larger place than they did in later times. The deities of the home, the dead ancestors, gave to the youthful state its solidity; in it, politics was a religion. But when the ideal in a measure disconnected man from his ancestors and made him act for, and more and more of, himself, religion and the tribe lost their supreme position. On the one hand, the Sophists, mirroring the popular mind, gave expression to the growing uncertainty about the gods. And on the other, Sophocles painted men and women as bringing the consequences of action upon themselves. The elders, it is true, discountenanced the Sophists, at bottom because, in response to the new ideal, the Sophists had put the individual before the state. Yet the bitterness of the attack of the elders is proof that they, too, felt in some measure the uneasiness of the times. The fears which the elders entertained for the religious safety of Greece received their fulfilment in their children. They and their descendants, the later Greeks, took up philosophy almost as their religion, and sought from its ethical teachings a reasonable guide for their conduct.

Religion — Development in Religious Thought

Even to the latest times, Homer was the moral and religious text-book of the young boys; but so far as its mythology was concerned, his poetry was, at a comparatively early time, in much the same regard that the legend of Santa Claus is to-day. It could not attempt to meet the religious needs of thinking men. Therefore the Mysteries were devised. "The greatest and best men of antiquity are unanimous in the opinion that they were created pure, and were intended to present high thoughts in an elevating way";[1] but it was not a great while before they degener-

In Religious Teaching

---
[1] Taylor: Eleusinian and Bacchic Mysteries.

ated, for the most part, into wild orgies. And none of the attempts to bring them back to their pristine vigor and purity restored them to their old position. That their teachings were always considered to be of great value is evident from the paramount question in times of danger, "Have you been initiated?" Yet, even in the times of the Sophists, to a much greater extent than we are accustomed to think, man had become "the measure of all things."

The ideal of personality, in religion as elsewhere, struck off every external restraint that held men down, and philosophy, springing from one's self, was made the guide. Socrates' daemon was the first expression of that newly-discovered control from within, which gradually obtained recognition.

To state this development in another form: In the early times, men trusted implicitly in the gods. In the transition period, as men came to realize the enormities of the Olympians, their beliefs were seriously shaken. And to this uncertainty the Sophists added their teachings of the changeability of all things, emphasizing meanwhile the excesses of the alleged divinities and spreading most skeptical views regarding them. Greek religion and the customary morality of Greece were thus, at the Attic period opposed, each to the other. And the Greek, as the result of a progessive movement strictly in accord with the new individualistic ideal, was left entirely at a loss for a firm foundation of belief. With the speculative nature peculiar to him, he was consequently ready to accept any teachings of philosophy which could afford him even the narrowest sure footing.

Reiteration

	CAUSALITY.	RELIGION
1	Worship of ancestors, Homeric religious conceptions,	Corresponds to place of family in ideal. Correspond to personal traits of the ideal.
2	Lowering of position of gods, . . Devising of mysteries, unrest, skepticism, and "man the measure of all things,"	Due to growth of political ideal. Due to growing consciousness of personality in the ideal.
3	Opposition of religion and morality, Socrates' daemon, and other similar recognitions of leading from within, ...	Due to ideal of perfection of personality. Due to same personal element in the ideal.
4	Adoption of philosophy for religion; Individual opinion and control,	Due to ideal of personal gratification and individual freedom.

Coming now to the customs of social life, we see again the same development. In the early organization of society, there was a class division into noblemen and freemen, on the basis of birth. The place of this was taken in the city-state by aristocracy and democracy, at first the survival of the old division, and later a distinction based on wealth. Finally, corresponding to an ideal which made every Greek a person, the whole citizen body was put on an equality before the law, in a pure democracy. (At various times aliens and slaves formed a large part of the population; but they did not belong to the citizen classes.)

Society — Caste Divisions

	CAUSALITY.	CASTE
1	Noblemen and freemen, based on birth, ...	Corresponds to physical ideal and to place of family in ideal.
2	Aristocracy and democracy, . .	Due to ideal of good as attained against others.
	Later division on wealth,	Due to growing consciousness of personality.
3 and 4	Democracy, .	Due to ideal of individual culture and perfection of personality.

(Subject classes correspond to and arise from Greek aristocratic ideal.)

The routine of ordinary life cannot vary much in its general outline. People must rise in the morning, and, at any rate, perform certain duties during the day. We find, however, a few changes in the course of Greek history. The table at which people sat in the early times gave way to the couch on which they reclined. The day, which was formerly passed at home, unless war engaged, was spent almost entirely away from home in the *agora*. And the public business which earlier filled the daytime so full, in the later times attracted but little disinterested attention. The business of society was the finding of its own enjoyment. The baths and the gymnasia were visited; the theater, too, entertained; and the day ended, perhaps, with revelling which made of the two days one.

Manner of Living

A notable characteristic of the early life was its hospitality, the institution of guest-friendship. This happy custom continued for many generations, but with the change of life from that of the tribe to the city organization, and with the development of state antagonism, two manifestations of a new ideal, it rapidly decayed. Only in rare instances, and among the old families, was it retained.

	CAUSALITY.	MANNER OF LIVING
1	All eating at table,	Corresponds to place of family in ideal.
	Day at home when not at war,	Same.
	Guest-friendship, . . .	Greek-ness of ideal; utilitarian element (?); family element.
2	Decay of guest-friendship, and	Due to ideal of good as attained against others.
3	Day in *agora* on public business, .	Due to citizen ideal.
4	Day in *agora* in search of enjoyment,	Due to ideal of personal gratification.
	Eating reclining, ...	To same, and ideal of elegance.

The accompaniments of the feasts in the earlier days were in keeping with the warlike ideal of an heroic race. Bards sang of the heroes, and of the gods who, in the likeness of men, helped their favorites in time of need. And ministering at once to the desire for entertainment and to the religious emotions, they stimulated and elevated the worthy men. But for the later times, with their desire for personal gratification, the glories of the gods and the heroes would not suffice, and effeminating and elaborate music and the mimes were introduced. The latter were, at first, dramatic performances in dialogue, but in the later times, they showed signs of the same degeneration that tainted other things, and ministered to the passions, rather than to the intellect and to the pure emotions. *(Festal Entertainments)*

	CAUSALITY.	ENTERTAINMENTS
1	Songs of heroes by bards, . .	Correspond to physical, external ideal.
2 and 3	Elaborate music, becoming effeminate, and mimes, . .	Due to ideal of individual culture with touch of following.
4	Degeneration of mimes and other forms of amusement, . .	Due to ideal of personal self-gratification.

The typical entertainments of Greece and the centers of her social life, aside from the *agora*, were the games and the theater. The former in the early days, and the latter in the palmy days of the empire, reached each its zenith. The great games were the Olympian, and at their quadrennial occurrence, men, both slave and free, noble and ignoble, flocked to Elis from all over Greece. Women alone — except the priestess of Demeter — were not allowed to be present. The festivals were primarily religious, and the same idea that made worship to the gods essential also fixed the character of that worship. Not only were there votive offerings to them, but the performance of the athletic exercises was in their honor. The *(The Games; Their Seriousness)* gods were thought to take delight in and command the sports. Yet this "sport" in itself was not like what we designate by the word to-day. The physical emphasis of the ideal, and the view of the gods as encouraging the sports *per se* — in reality the second is the manifestation of the presence of the first — gave to the games a seriousness which it is hard for us to imagine. The strength of hereditary custom kept this seriousness alive long after the ideal had lost its former power. But gradually it, too, was lost, and so much did the games change in character, and so notorious did they become, that Cicero resented as an insult the statement that he was present at their celebration.

Pan-Hellenic in their nature, these festivals were an outgrowth of the Greek spirit. The ideal of the Greeks as equal made all Greeks, and no one else, eligible to competition; and victory was esteemed the great honor, not of the winner only, but of his state.

Character of the Contests

The growing subjectivity of the ideal was paralleled by a change in the character of the contests. At first limited to the foot-race, and then to the contests of the trumpeters and to foot-races, wrestling matches, and the pentathlon, there were gradually introduced trials of skill which called for training of the eye and ear. A contest in music developed quite early from that of the trumpeters; there were contests in poetry and in the arts; and the philosophers went to the games to discuss their doctrines — perhaps to dispute, if there were any who opposed them. Chariot races, too, were introduced, affording great opportunity for display, and making it possible also for one to win the wreath, not by personal ability, but by wealth. The final stage of this growing consciousness is seen in the dramatic contests at Athens, which have given us the trilogies of Aeschylus, Sophocles, and Euripides.

	CAUSALITY.	GAMES
1	Religious festivals and seriousness,	Correspond to place of family and religion in ideal.
	Only Hellenic, but Pan-Hellenic,	To Greek-ness of ideal.
	Only athletic contests,	To physical ideal.
2	Introduction of skilled contests,	Due to intellectual growth in the ideal.
	Chariot races,	Due to consciousness of personality growing, and to mercenary tendency (which may only be a side of this).

3 and 4 Loss of seriousness,	Due to loss of place of family and religion in ideal, *i. e.*, growing personality.
Dramatic contests, . .	Due to new ideal of individual culture
And in their evolution, to ideal of personal self-gratification.	

The stage of Athens was also typical, and in the later days was marked by all the disgraces which might be seen in the streets. Some declare that the characteristic representations set forth do not necessarily show an evil society, or one totally vitiated; that the Athenians were well taught by example, by the sight of that which is evil and its consequences to avoid it. It may be so, and we will gladly make all the allowance we can for unusual intellectual abilities, even in the very young, so that they might not linger on the details of any of the scenes enacted, but hold in memory only the truth which they portrayed. But we are constrained to think that it was not the teachings of the Sophists that undermined Greek morality, so much as the corrupt mythology and the sensual productions of the theater. While a few saw underneath the symbols the great principle whose inculcation may have been intended, the great multitude beheld chiefly representations which gratified the senses, and seemed to them to justify immorality.[1] For in their ideal of personal freedom, as we already have said more than once, the element of necessary restraint was largely wanting. *The Theater*

In the sketches which history has left us of the Athenian society of these times, there is material for a dark picture. Judicial trials had never been conducted on what we to-day should call principles of justice, and the arbitrariness of the old council and the chief who presided over it still existed. But to this there was added, not the previous bias of honor and consideration of the public good, but a large item of personal gain. Bribery was common, and for the most part uncondemned, unless it was to the positive detriment of the state; and even then it was not much more than frowned upon. The good man was identified with the one who had wealth with which to provide for his pleasure. Gloss them over as we may, the licentiousness, the openly recognized *hetairae*, the preva- *Athenian Society about 430 B.C.*

---

[1] Duruy: History of Greece, i: 431.

lence of irreligion, the extravagance, and, withal, the laziness of Athens were unknown to the Greeks of the previous ages. Sumptuary laws were passed from time to time. The maximum number of guests at an evening entertainment and the expense of those entertainments were determined by law. The highest allowed amount of individual fortune was fixed, and laws were passed attacking the general improvidence; but without effect. The condition of Athens about 430 has few parallels in history. It was a combination of the very highest intellectual attainment in the field of philosophy and theoretical morality with the greatest inherent wickedness and badness. Plato is admirably pictured by Benn in his "Greek Philosophers" as a moral reformer, but coming even forty years later, when its previous fury had been reduced, he could not stem the tide. It still swept on, and only as they suited the popular cry, in perverted Epicureanism, did his doctrines touch the common life. Later Athenian society, however, shows on the whole a gradual ascent, and a slow recuperation in the ethics of individual living. There is the appearance of a certain approach to soundness which corresponds to the Hellenic ideal.

Development of Other Customs

A few customs which we have not yet noted show, on the whole, an advance from the time of Homer in the recognition of the rights of humanity. In the early days the orphan had no rights which people must respect; he was robbed of his patrimony and abandoned by those who had been his father's friends; but in Athens there were special laws for the protection of the persons and property of orphan minors. To them, as well as to all other Greek-born residents, the new ideal guaranteed a measure of security. It was customary for the heroes to pierce with spears the bodies of those slain in battle, and to offer them all sorts of indignities; but by reason of the new ideal of personality, for an Athenian of the Age of Pericles to maltreat in any way the body of an enemy was a deep disgrace, even though it might appear to find some justification in circumstances. So the right of private revenge on the murderer, which had belonged to every man as against the wrong-doer, was exchanged for orderly trial by jury, which acknowledged rights on both sides. The crime was not thought of chiefly as a deed of violence, but as an act against the city and the gods.

Pending judgment, the accused was interdicted from worship and from public places, and if found guilty of entering the forbidden enclosures, he was sentenced by the state to death or banishment. Again, this turning to unity, by which the city was foremost in thought, brought it about that the order of battle was no longer single combat, but the onset or defence of a disciplined army. Likewise, the head of the state was no longer simply the leader and the "shepherd of the people," but the wise and astute legislator, who maintains a preconcerted system of laws.

IV — PARALLEL DEVELOPMENT OF INSTITUTIONS RELATING TO INDIVIDUAL CULTURE[1]

There is one line of development at which we have not yet looked, and it is of great importance, that in the education of the youth of Greece. In the early days, the training of childhood was under the care of the mother, to keep the boys from contamination and to rear successive generations of pure Greeks. At the family hearth, they were taught the worship of the gods, and acquired the general, fundamental knowledge necessary for life. The education of youth was largely for war. The muscles were hardened, and keenness of sight and accuracy of aim cultivated in the chase. Young men also learned the use of the common implements, and were often skillful players on the *cithera*. But in the early culture, so largely physical, there was small play for, and therefore little education of, the intellect. We may say, with almost literal truth, it was not known. Moral teaching was largely by example. The ideal of courage and of bravery in combat was early inculcated, and it was enforced by the approval of the family and the gods.

In the period of transition, education became more and more intellectual, and moral teaching was by precept as well as example. There was a growing demand for scientific knowledge. Greek adventurers brought back from other lands many new facts. On the one hand, the sages attempted from these materials daringly to reconstruct the universe, and as, on the other, they looked out on life, their thinking shaped itself in maxims for the guidance of conduct. No longer was the object

Transitional and Attic — Instruction

---

[1] For a thorough consideration, see Davidson: Aristotle and Early Educational Ideals.

of instruction the simple training of warriors. The man of whom every boy was conceived to be the father was a citizen, fully able to perform his duties as such, both in war and in peace. So the physical training became systematic, under the care of a director and in a public gymnasium. There was a careful course of work, the end of which was strength and symmetry of development, together with grace and ease of movement.

Homer was the text-book which each boy learned by heart, and from which, primarily, his moral ideas were drawn. The action of the epic, as we have taken occasion to remark in our study of the ideal, is decidedly utilitarian; and so the boy was tacitly trained to do certain things as customary, and certain others as bringing him advantages. Yet there was a moral vein in the teaching. Whereas, in Sparta, boys were instructed to steal, if they could do so without being found out, in the Athenian gymnasium, the theft of any article above ten *drachmae* in value was punished, not by any light penalty, but by death (so authoritative were made thus early in life the laws and the welfare of the state).

Teachers In this transition period, the instruction was at home and private, if not as by a private tutor, yet not more common than that of a "select" school. But toward the end of the first period came the Sophists, the first University teachers and the precursors of the public schools. The pressing demand was for men competent to train a higher type of citizen than the mere soldier— the *ephebus* of the Spartans, able to obey orders unquestioningly but not to think intelligently for himself — and to satisfy this they had arisen. The object was now to fit men for the understanding and proper execution of political affairs. The Sophists were shrewd men, and, understanding the situation, undertook to fulfill the present want and nothing more. Traveling all over Greece, they carried to the youths simply the learning of which they themselves had become possessed, and discussed with them matters relating to common life. These teachers have been likened in their office to our newspapers, and the education which they afforded was of much the same character, relating to the topics of the day and practical. Their training was also somewhat like that of the college "coach." They gave mainly a superficial knowledge, but it met the demand.

In their teachings, the Sophists soon developed specialties, and urged the value of certain accomplishments which are the results, rather than the essence, of true learning and culture. The elders, as guardians of the state, naturally attacked them, for much learning had somewhat unbalanced the minds of these rhetoricians, and they taught doubt and contingency in everything, to the real subversion of morality and good citizenship. To the deep thinkers, their shallowness too, was probably somewhat disgusting. But we should not estimate them below their real worth, and so fall into the error which we ourselves criticise. On the whole, they were a class of investigators highly deserving the honor which was given them by some, though they were with reason maligned by others. Socrates differed from them in that he taught something to take the place of that which he had removed; he was a constructive, as well as a destructive thinker. Unfortunately, men of his stamp were not the typical instructors of Athenian youth. Yet, they all, in their elevation of the individual mind, made their teachings correspond to the predominant ideal of personality.

In still later times, the education was in large degree physical, but the previous object of development was not active. The end was refinement and dilettanteism. Grace and enjoyment were most sought in physical development and gymnastic exercise. Whereas these had been more or less objects of admiration, they now became ends of action. In intellectual culture, for the majority, the aim was success in rhetorical debate, and personal gain through the contests of the dicastery. An important educational factor of these times was the schools of the philosophers. They show the continued working of the subjective ideal, and are characteristic of the intellectual bent of the Greek mind. So far as the general morality of the people is concerned, the schools seem to have exercised an elevating influence, and had Athens retained her independence, there was still the moral foundation for a very high civilization. But as a subject state, the incentives to revolution were not many; moreover, the creative strength and virility of the race seem to have been spent. The Athenians were content to live on in culture. Though no longer aggressive, their education in its apparent object, much more than that of any previous age, made for the

Hellenic

training of the individual personality in all its spheres, as it was understood by the great philosophers. The doctrines of the schools, reduced somewhat and diluted for the popular comprehension, attained a real influence in Greek life, and they present, in their realization, perhaps the most cultured type of Greek history, a man thoroughly "refined," though not particularly virile.

	CAUSALITY.	EDUCATION
	(Education is simply the leading out of life to correspond to the ideal.)	
1	Education at home,	Corresponds to place of family in ideal.
	Religious,	To place of religion in ideal and thus indirectly to the same.
	For war, by chase, physical,	To physical ideal.
	Emphasis on bravery,	Shows effect of same ideal.
	Morality taught in example,	Shows same ideal.
2	Private instruction, decreasing,	To decreasing place of family in ideal.
2 and 3	More intellectual scientific knowledge, morality by precept,	To intellectual growth of ideal.
	Politico-utilitarian morality,	Due to political ideal.
	Systematic public gymnasia, to train citizens,	Due to same.
	Sophists,	Due to ideal of individual culture.
4	For grace and enjoyment,	Due to ideal of pleasure.
	Rhetorical success and personal gain,	To ideal of self-gratification.
	Schools of philosophers,	Due to ideal of personality in its better elements.

V — OTHER PARALLEL DEVELOPMENTS

There are other phenomena which exhibit the same development of the ideal, although, in strictness, they do not fall under the head of institutions.

Music

Music, in the early days, while in itself a slave to words, was in its character martial and in its effects stimulating. In the middle period, perhaps because of the new emotional element which it was called on to portray, it became somewhat effeminate. At first this tendency was sharply rebuked; the seductive strains,

"Softly sweet in Lydian measure,"

were thought to disturb and endanger morality. But, in the later days, the tunes were for the most part light and with the intent of giving pleasure; and the softness which had met with so cold a reception was now passed over in silence, or, mayhap, it was loudly welcomed.

In literature, in the early period, comporting with the externality of the ideal, we find tales relating to the heroic deeds of battle or to the actions of the personified forces of nature. The middle period with its growing interest in man, although yet occupied with the manifestation of his self, rather than with that self itself, expressed its feelings in lyrics, half moral, which are best fitted to mirror a life chiefly consisting in emotions and actions. The typical writing of the later period is that in which the subjectivity of the ideal finds its fullest expression, philosophic prose. From this, the advance is to criticism, rather than creation, in all departments. Between the lyrics and philosophy stand the dramatic monuments, combining the expression of the emotions of human nature with the introspective relation of the facts of man's self-consciousness. *Literature*

There is this same development in ethical theory and in the nature of philosophy. The Homeric men looked out on life without any very definitely recognized theory of conduct. They did, in general, what came first to hand. Next, the sages laid down their maxims of morality; but these were from a popular point of view, and were the outcome of the lives of individual men, rather than the expression of any system. In the Periclean Age, we have moral teaching which is to some extent systematic; yet it was largely the expression of men's own personalities, as is seen, for instance, in Socrates' incarnation of his own theory. Later, there were the regulated systems of ethical thought, founded on Aristotle's Ethics. The Stoics and Epicureans, each securing a half-truth, erected it into a systematic guide of conduct. *Ethics*

So too, early philosophy was a cosmology; man tried to harmonize surrounding nature. The first step from this was to man's actions. The early question as to nature received a final answer from Leucippus,[1] and of necessity, man became the subject of inquiry. This investigation had first to do with his outward action; then it became introspective and psychological, reaching below the surface to the springs of action. Its later expression was in the criticism of pre-existing theories, and not in the creation of new ones. *Philosophy*

---
[1] Burnet: Early Greek Philosophy.

In the three great dramatists, we have this same progress repeated in miniature. Aeschylus is the portrayer of the ideal of the past. The great forces are those of nature, and the inexorable Fates determine the bounds of mortal life. The view is altogether outward; the characteristic excellences are those of the heroes. The moral teachings are after the manner of those of the sages. Sophocles depicts idealized persons; he represents man as bringing the punishments of action upon himself. He is typical of the new psychological school of thinkers, to which also belong Thucydides and the three philosophers. They investigate man's nature, and put into practice the Socratic motto, "Know thyself." Euripides is critical, morose, and peevish; he presents man as enervated, and there is a noticeable decline in the strength of individual action.

The Three Great Dramatists

We may find the early and late stages of Greece illustrated, in their general aspects, in the contemporary life of Athens and Sparta 450–400 B. C. Spartan policy held to the old customs, and as much as possible, kept Spartans separate from the rest of the Greeks. A small state, watched over by officials of a common mind in this regard, was able, for many generations, to keep its primitive form, in spite of the workings of the ideal in the minds of the people. Among the subject Helots, the most progressive were promptly dispatched, their assassination furnishing the youths, the future guardians of the state, with their first practical instruction in the tactics to be pursued. In those who were born Spartans, the spirit of progress was repressed by education and custom. The Spartan ideal was the citizen, always ready for war, and a member of a state which depended upon war for its prestige.

Sparta and Athens as Typical of Early and Later Stages

On the other hand, what was the Athenian ideal? There are some who maintain that the Spartan warrior and the Spartan matron were the ideal of all the Greeks, including the Athenians. We do not think this is correct. For, in the first place, some say that the life of the city, *i. e.*, of Athens, was more typical of Greece than the soldier life and the severe training of Sparta. In fact, the Spartans boasted that they alone of all the Greeks had held true to the old ideal. Then, too, the ideal of the Athenian had a deeper content than that of the Spartan; the ideal of the latter was of physical development, and he fulfiled it. No doubt the Athenian admired the superb strength and the endurance of the Spartan youths, and perhaps their great filial devotion and respect for old age. But what they admired was not therefore their ideal. Who shall say that many an Athenian youth, while with his eyes he watched the actions of those bitter rivals of his city, was not mentally thankful that the gods or the fates or some kind providence had spared him the rigors and severities of the Spartan discipline? No, the ideals of the two were different. While all the rest of Greece, and Athens in particular, had been moving forward, Sparta had remained practically still. Now she stood alone, the mark of a past type of manhood and of human civilization, a sort of milestone to tell men that civilization in its march had passed that way. And finally the change which had come in the other states came here also, with the great upheaval of civil war. But it was too late, and now the new ideal was not able to attain adequate manifestation. While down along the ages and, indeed, to-day, in this nineteenth century and this new-found world, the memory of Athens is richly fragrant because of her additions, even to our Western life, Sparta is remembered only as are those who by their ill-success exhort men not to follow in their footsteps.

This is not the place for a digression on the evil of repressing the free working and manifestation of the ideal of a people, but there are some quite apparent lessons which may be drawn from this comparative development, and with considerable profit.

For Summary, see following chart:

INSTITUTIONS RELATING TO

PERIOD	IDEAL	Subjugation of Nature		Social Organization				Social Customs			Individual Culture	Other Parallel Developments
		Material Welfare	Common Occupations	Family	State	Religion	Caste	Life	Amusements	Sports	Education	
Homeric —700 B.C.	**Warrior**; bravery, physical excellence. Member of family (preferably noble). Activity; for advantage. External; unconscious.	Sort of com. fort. Rude splendor.	Warrior and farmer. All work.	Homeric family; primary bond of society; monogamous; public marriage ceremony. Women on equality with men; purity of life.	Homeric State; patriarchal community; mutual responsibility (natural government). Amphictyonic League.	Physical and external religious conceptions. Worship of ancestors.	Noblemen and freemen. Based on birth.	All ate at table. Day at home.	Songs of heroes by bards.	Athletic festivals; religious; serious.	For war by chase; physical. In childhood at home; by mother; religious. Morality by example.	1 Music martial, and stirring. 2 Epic poetry. 3 Morality = practical life. 4 Philosophy cosmological. 5 Æschylus typical. 6 Sparta typical.
Transitional 700-450 cir.	**Warrior-Citizen**; increasingly political. To be attained against others; calling for victory. Growing in line of individual culture and gain. External.	Growing comfort.	City affairs. Getting rich.	Losing regard for family. Women secluded.	Loss of power of family. City-State; primary bond of society. Oligarchy and tyranny. Class agitations. Hegemonies.	Skepticism; man the measure. Lowering of position of gods. Mysteries; unrest.	Aristocracy and Democracy. Division by wealth.	Decay of guest-friendship.	More elaborate music. Becoming effeminate.	Skilled contests. Chariot races.	More intellectual. Decrease in private instruction. Systematic public gymnasium work. Object; to train citizens. Morality by precept. The Sophists.	1 Effeminate music; rebuked. 2 Lyrics and the Drama. 3 Experimental morality and precepts. 4 Philosophy *de* external side of conduct.
Attic 450 cir.—400.	**Citizen**; 1 Individual culture in state; 2 advancement of state; 2 individual culture and gain; 3 development of personality. Increasingly self-conscious.	Greater magnificence.	Affairs of state. Getting rich.	Same; women degraded; *hetairai*. Corruption of 430.	Democracy; tyranny of people. Liberty.	Opposition of religion and morality. Socrates, δαίμων.	Democracy and subject classes.	Day in *agora* on public business.	Mimes.	Dramatic contests. Loss of seriousness.	The same continuing. Object; to fit men to understand and execute political affairs.	1 Much light music. 2 Philosophic prose. 3 Morality systematic but personal. 4 Philosophy *de* Ethics and rudimentary Psychology. 5 Sophocles typical. 6 Athens typical.
Hellenic 400—	**Athenian Gentleman**; refinement, elegance, and ease. Personal gratification and freedom. Something of self-control. Self-conscious.	Luxuriousness.	Use of leisure; support at public expense; gain; pleasure-seeking. Artisans looked down on.	Glossing over of evil crowd. Degradation; but some betterment.	Catering of rulers to crowd. Political apathy; corruption; withdrawal of old families from politics. Conquest. Achæan League.	Philosophy for religion. Individual opinion and control.	Democracy and subject classes.	Day in *agora* in search of enjoyment. Eating reclining.	Degeneration of mimes and other forms of amusement.	—	For grace and enjoyment; rhetorical success and personal gain. Schools of Philosophy.	1 Music effeminating to give greatest pleasure. 2 Criticism. 3 Moral Philosophy. 4 Philosophy = criticism of previous theories. 5 Euripides typical.

CHAPTER II

THE PARALLEL DEVELOPMENT OF ROMAN IDEALS AND INSTITUTIONS

If we may believe tradition, Rome sprang into existence through the direct efforts of an organized band of men. The founding of the city was not the origin of a fresh civilization, but the formation of a new community on the basis of the preceding Etruscan order. For some time, then, institutions should correspond very closely to the ideal, as its specific manifestations.

I — THE DEVELOPMENT OF THE IDEAL

The early ideal demanded above all else the service and defence of the state. Patriotism was the great duty; to the welfare of the city the ideal man would sacrifice everything. The virtue, the energy, the confidence of Rome all flowed in this one channel. Yet the times when war did not summon were not spent in ease. Then the ideal man tilled his farm, for he was full of activity. *Early Roman Ideal*

Closely interwoven with devotion to the state was the maintenance of the family and the gens. Here the ideal called not simply for the rearing of a family; it made the hearth the father's throne, and the ideal man was as much the unquestioned ruler in the *familia*, as he was the obedient servant in the state.

So far as the gods were concerned, the ideal man had their help. When he asked for their aid, he did so with vows which he was very careful to keep; and, indeed, he never broke his oath, either with the gods or with men.

In private life the ideal called for morality and virtue. And to the virtue there attached that military flavor which its derivation from the word meaning hero, *vir*, would indicate. Manhood was rude and passionate, but sturdy.

To put this in fewer words: The ideal man of early Rome

was a Roman citizen, glorying in his name and desiring the maintenance of the Roman line, therefore the head of a family; devoted to the defence of Rome, whose call had power over him above all else, therefore a warrior. In the family he was a despot, but in the state the subject of the common will. In time of peace his pursuit was husbandry. His virtue was in fighting bravely for the defence of Rome, in upholding his gens and family, in keeping faith with the gods and with his fellows, and in living in purity and frugality. So Duruy declares[1] that the sum of virtues in these early Romans was *virtus et pietas;* and these two called for courage and force, for immoveable firmness and for patience in work, for respect to the gods, the ancestors, and the fatherland, the family, and the established laws and discipline.

It is difficult, in the centuries which immediately follow, to trace a chronological development of the ideal.

Chronological Development

If we regard the early period as extending to the beginning of the plebeian struggles and the secession to the Sacred Mount in 494 B. C., we see next, in the history of institutions, a strife between patricians and plebeians which lasts till 286. But so far as the ideal is concerned, this does not seem to have been a period of great change. We note that at its close the maintenance of the glory of Rome had passed out of the hands of the old families into those of the common people. But their ideal seems to have been much the same as that of those who to them were the old Romans, and future generations looked back to these plebeians as the incarnation of what they in turn called the old Roman virtues. In the class strife, however, while all were ready to answer the call to the defence of Rome, there was a strong union of individual good with the success of the party, as well as with that of the state. When the contest was over there was practically one party — the aggressive and politically-minded plebs. But the idea in which the party and the state were one with the individual end of action soon made a differentiation, and while at the summit of the Republic — from 286 to the end of the Punic wars, setting thus an arbitrary date, 146 — everything seemed in the best condition, there was a change working underneath.

---

[1] Duruy: History of Rome, i: 140.

There may be, in the acts which emanate from them, but little apparent difference between an ideal of the state as the sum of all action and all individual ends, and an ideal calling for the aggrandizement of the state. But there is a real difference, which is perhaps most manifest in the extent to which self-sacrifice is a part of the ideal. There is no question as to the presence of this in the early ideal. The state was above all. Brutus gave up his sons that the laws of the commonwealth might not be overridden and that its authority might be sustained. It is true that we see the same thing in the Punic wars, that Regulus and other citizens, like true heroes, gave up themselves and their own for the defence of the state. But they were increasingly thought of as belonging to the old school. The spirit of conquest was not that of defence. When the spring of action is not patriotism primarily, but aggrandizement, it may at first center in the state, but the steps are not difficult by which its nature changes to the aggrandizement of family and then of self. So the ideal did not demand virtuous living so much as it demanded that which was honorable; and, unfortunately, between the two there may be considerable difference. As far as individual morality was concerned, there was little, if any, immediate change. But the important thing is that there had been a slight change in the character of the ideal, one which was growing, and which made its appearance in the luxurious selfishness and the civil dissensions of the later days.

<small>Latent Change</small>

The next period we date from the conquest of the Mediterranean, in 146, to the accession of Augustus, B. C. 29. This was really a time of transition in the ideal as well as in politics. The idea of good operative in men's minds was of personal gain, the outgrowth which the slight change in the third century foreshadowed. Of its gradual manifestation we shall be able to speak at length under the head of institutions. Suffice it now to say, that the struggle was not for honorable citizenship. Lucilius declares, "To-day gold holds the place of virtue, and by what thou hast thy worth will be measured." Mommsen says that "the preservation and increase of wealth positively became a part of the public morality," and that

<small>Ideal of the Later Republic</small>

"deep-rooted immorality ate into the heart of the commonwealth, and substituted an absolute selfishness for humanity and patriotism."[1] Any one of the triumvirs is in large measure typical of the aims and ideals of this epoch. Men sought power and pleasure, and the pursuit of either brought in its train the evils and corruptions of immorality. The desire was for luxury and display, and for sensual enjoyment. Men lamented the ancient virtues, but they cared not for them. Men talked like Cato, but they lived as did Lucullus. The ideal was not of a person guided or restrained in his actions; control of any kind was a species of nightmare, of which men wished with all their hearts to be rid; and yet they did not value political liberty, and without objection they saw it vanish. The sphere of life in which they asked license was left to them, but they lost the vastly more important freedom, of which but few of them were aware.

Here we pause to review the parallel development of Roman institutions, for with the early empire, or, indeed, before it, the Roman character was lost. The ideal of the Greeks had its influence, in company with that of other nations, and we have no longer Rome, but the Roman world. From the time of the first contact of Rome with Greece this had been true in increasing measure, and now the moral unit was not any one nation, but the empire.

II — PARALLEL DEVELOPMENT OF INSTITUTIONS RELATING TO THE SUBJUGATION OF NATURE

Material Welfare — Buildings

Had it been our privilege some day to step into early Rome, the antiquarians tell us that we would have found a town laid out very irregularly, and composed of thatched huts — save a few buildings of a better class, those dedicated to the worship of the national divinities. This was the condition of things down to the sack of Rome by Brennus. When the people returned from their enforced exodus, the town was rebuilt on a larger and more respectable scale, but in the same irregular manner. Still the public buildings were far better and more imposing than the homes of the citizens. In fact, men gloried in their rude habitations, contrasting so strongly

---

[1] Mommsen: History of Rome, ii: 454, 460.

with the stately and magnificent senate chamber. The city of the dead bore, too, the same marks; the tombs were small and without ornaments to attract attention. In the plans of the houses the windows were in the second story, and would seem to indicate a certain seclusion, the reflex of the carefully guarded home-life of the republic. This is the "city of brick and wood." It did not, however, retain its "provincial" character. The immense plunder which flowed into the capital from the foreign wars became visible in the buildings of the city. Already, at the time of the second Punic war, some houses bore the marks of the luxury of Tarentum, and we read that the tomb of the Scipios was decorated in the fashion of the Greek art. Thenceforth the *domi* of the well-to-do grew more and more elegant, and the dwellings of the rich became very ostentatious. Not that there was no corresponding change in the public buildings — in 131, a certain Metellus erected a temple entirely of marble — but there was not the contrast which had formerly been marked between the homes of the citizens and the residences of the glory of the nation.

This tendency to enrich individual environment appears in the decoration of the houses. Until the time of the Punic wars, art had been sacerdotal and connected with the beautifying of the temples; but now it turned to the amenities of common life, and sought to make them more pleasing by adding to the beauty of their surroundings. It would seem that the walls of almost all dwellings bore decorations of some kind in colors. Landscapes and pictures of still-life were common, and there have been found many figure paintings which show the influence of the Greek innovations. In the time of Augustus the development reached a great height of luxury. The decorations of many buildings were of ivory and marble, valuable woods and precious stones. The magnificence of private houses was such as to excite more and more prominent mention, and in place of the simple tombs there were the ornate mausolea and moles.

Decorations

There are two things which show us the parallelism of this change with the development of the ideal; the beautiful and costly ornaments were had, not because they were the best, and so would be more useful than any others, nor because of their intrinsic value, but rather for the display their owner could thus make and the notoriety they would bring him. And of the pictures and decorations of the wall, one historian says with commendable briefness, "they were often of a character exceedingly unfavorable to purity of mind."

<small>Luxury</small>
The same tendency to luxuriousness is seen in matters pertaining to food and drink. In the early days the fare was frugal and life in all its aspects was hard and austere. So it continued for a long time, but the sudden increase of riches smoothed the way to new comforts and to extravagance. What had been to some extent a question of conscience was evidently now a matter of poverty only. Meals grew more and more elaborate. Formerly there had been only one warm meal a day; now the *prandium* also was warm, and the *cœna* was no longer limited to two courses. Of some persons it is related that they had seven courses, and dined alone. Men did not sit at meals as formerly, but, according to the Greek custom, they reclined, and the *triclinarium* was made one of the pleasantest rooms in the house. The banqueting hall was most sumptuously furnished. Great extravagance was displayed in the appointments of the table, and in the settings and accompaniments of the feast expense seems to have been disregarded. For a dinner 25,000 sesterces was not considered an excessive amount, and for an ordinary meal the outlay was by no means small.

These things, however, were not allowed to continue without protest, for at first they were affected by only the "Four Hundred" of Rome. The body of the people did not share them, and were, indeed, opposed to them, as they showed by the sumptuary laws which they enacted. It was in these earlier days that Cato announced his intention of dealing with these follies by law, should he be elected censor; and he did not forget his declaration when he found himself in office. He and his party seem to have conserved Roman frugality and virtue to a considerable degree, but striking at symptoms rather than at the root of the disease, they could not effect a cure. So there were, all along, some who saw the evils of luxury and tried to stem the tide, but as the people, and not the nobility alone, gradually became involved, as the people adopted the ideal of self-gratification, they were able to accomplish less and less — for the people had chosen against them.

The facts regarding the luxuriousness of the later days of the Republic are, in themselves, enough to occupy a volume. The richness and ostentation of private houses, both within and without, the massive ornaments of the vehicles, the change in dress both of men and of women (against which Cato protested so vehemently after the second Punic war), the example of the languid Crispinus, who had a set of finger rings for winter wear, and because, forsooth, they were too heavy, some of lighter weight for the hot summer — these are only samples. The more we study the period, the more we are compelled to agree with Livy, when he says, "Nevertheless, those innovations which were then (second Punic war) looked on as remarkable were scarcely even the seeds of future luxury." [1]

This Luxury only a Beginning

If we were reading with an eye jealous for the glory of Rome, there are two facts here which ought to make us very solicitous. Both of them show the spread of the new ideal. The luxury at which we are later astonished was introduced into the city, not by foreigners, nor by the rabble of Rome, nor by Roman women. It was brought in by her soldiers, those who in their frugality and hardiness had been the foundation of her greatness. Then, too, the object of the new development was not simply comfort. If it was that at first, it soon passed to the love of enjoyment and to the desire for display. It had been a virtue of the early Roman life that it was real — as it was, so it appeared; but now the early simplicity was gone, and with it its reality. Life was almost a sham; the important thing was to keep up appearances and to surpass one's fellows in display. Indeed, the one great end, the object of an expensive dinner, was that the name of its giver might be on every one's lips. How unlike the rivalries of their sturdy ancestors for honor and renown on the hard-fought field of battle. But, mayhap, their ancestors did not fight for Rome, and they themselves are not of Roman blood!

Two Reasons for Solicitude as to the Future of Rome

---
[1] Livy, xxxviii : 6.

CAUSALITY.	MATERIAL WELFARE
1 Poor dwellings and imposing public buildings,	Correspond to ideal of devotion to the state.
Tombs unornamented, art sacerdotal,	To same.
Frugal living,	To same.
Seclusion of house,	To ideal of virtuous, pure living; to place of family in ideal.
1 *c.* Loss of contrast,	Due to ideal of family and personal aggrandizement.
Tombs decorated, art in homes,	To same.
Growing comfort, elaborateness, and display — among only a few in this period,	To ideal of gain, and growing ideal of enjoyment and display.
1 and 2 Ostentatious and elegant homes,	Due to ideal of display.
Decorations the same and immoral,	Due to same, and to ideal of sensual selfish gratification.
Costly and elaborate meals, little opposition,	Due to same.

Occupations — Early

In early Rome there were two occupations, war and agriculture; and of the two, war was the chief. Every man expected to work, to do something; but he was ready to drop everything else at the call of the city for his services in war. Cincinnatus, leaving his plow for the dictatorship, and returning again to the field when he had led the Roman arms to speedy victory, is typical of this early spirit in which patriotism was the highest motive. And this was the *animus* of every freeman. No standing army then was needed, for every citizen was a soldier.

Developments in the Army

This was the condition of things till about the time of the Samnite wars; but then a new period was entered upon. The army no longer existed for defence alone; it was for conquest. The military formation was changed, and the swift-moving legion took the place of the formidable but heavy phalanx. Instead of the citizen militia, there was a standing army of paid soldiery, and while to call them mercenaries, though technically correct, would by our ordinary understanding be wrong, this is what the legions soon became. There was, at the same time, a change in the temper of military obedience. To the early Romans war was a duty, but to the soldiers of the later republic it was a business; in its essence it was a traffic in plunder. The early soldiers were great in their devotion to the commonwealth, and their patriotism was impersonal, a love for native land. The soldier of the legion, however, was busy in foreign campaigns, in which success was largely dependent upon the

will and ability of the commander, and the end was plunder and
the glory of the general and his army. So devotion, while perhaps, as yet, not less hearty, was to the leader rather than to the
state. The veterans of the army of Marius or of Sulla were
the veterans of their respective commanders, while, for instance,
those of Cato in Spain were the old soldiers of Rome or of the
Spanish campaign. Corresponding to both these was the
almost imperceptible change which had come over Roman
strategics. At first, and for many years, the prowess of the
soldiers, their strength and bravery, had decided the battle.
But gradually craft was recognized as having a place in the arts
of war, and men sought to defeat the enemy by deception,
rather than by overpowering his forces.

With the establishment of a standing army, we see the
Roman citizen turn his attention to other pursuits. Agriculture continued all along to be highly honorable; it was the occupation which poets and literary men delighted to extol. But the trades and handicrafts were looked down on. Wholesale commerce was thought to be respectable, for there was considerable money in it, although retail trade was lightly esteemed. Money lenders had a large income, but their business was unsavory. "Lending money at interest has various advantages, but it is not honorable," was the general opinion. Yet these men played an important part in the building up of Rome. Politics furnished quite a field for one's exertions. Many thought it worth their while to fit themselves for public life, and in various capacities rendered their country much service and gained for themselves either the esteem or the deadly hatred of their fellow-citizens. Yet barriers were here interposed, by provisions which made the curule ædileship the stepping-stone to higher offices, and then, by making it the ædile's duty to give magnificent games at his own expense, shut out from political advancement all who were not of great wealth. Whereas, in the early state, idleness had been the exception, in the later republic it became the rule. And unfortunately, while the men of that day did not feel disposed to work, to beg they were by no means ashamed. Such institutions as the later clientage, the *sportula*, the *captatores*, the *Leges Frumentarii*, show plainly their servility. In the last days of the

Other Pursuits in the Later Republic

republic, the honorable pursuits may be summed up in these: to enjoy one's self, to live upon the bounty of some friend or patron, to receive the income from one's landed estates or to superintend them in person, to be busy in intellectual pursuits, to invest one's money in trading and in the provinces, and, perhaps, to dabble in politics, although this last was dangerous. In all these, excepting politics and intellectual pursuits, it is apparent that life lacked any deep and serious purpose. And if, as to these two, we recall that politics was very largely a game of self-interest, and that the great mass of literary activity was for the sake of applause, it is not difficult to see the correspondence of the occupations of this time to an ideal of selfish gratification and display.

Looking out from Rome in these times we see a deplorable condition of things. The city ideal of personal pleasure had worked great harm outside, as well as within, her walls. The small farmers of the Italian plains had given up their plots of ground, because there was no encouragement to them to continue. Wheat could be bought in Rome, thanks to the corn laws, cheaper than they could raise it. In economic as well as other lines, everything was sacrificed to what were thought to be the interests of the population of the capital, and for them bread never could be too cheap. So the disheartened peasant, attracted by stories of the city's life as the moth is by the candle's flame, gave up his few *jugera* and went to Rome. His land was incorporated in the estate of some wealthy land-owner, and the work on it was done by slaves. The rustic, who is ever the hope of the state, now lived on its bounty, instead of contributing to its maintenance; and with the servility which he soon acquired by imitation, and with the constant excitements provided for the city populace, his manhood presently disappeared. Once he had stood distinct as a unit, he and all his fellows, each a pillar under Rome, but now his identity was lost in the heterogeneous mass, the city rabble. And the change which had come about in his condition corresponded again to the growing ideal of individual gratification and of personal enjoyment.

Condition of Things in Italy

CASUALITY.	COMMON OCCUPATIONS
1 War,	Corresponds to ideal of devotion to the state.
Agriculture,	To same, supporting its life and that of the family.
1c Army for conquest, phalanx to legion, war a business,	Due to ideal of aggrandizement.
1 and 2 New strategies,	To same, and ideal of gain.
Agriculture, and wholesale, rather than retail, commerce,	To ideal of honorable living.
Outcry against money-lenders,	To same, and citizen ideal.
2 Devotion to general,	To ideal of personal gain and aggrandizement.
Condition of politics as business,	To ideal of family and self-aggrandizement.
Rustic in city rabble,	To ideal of gratification on part of city ; of gain on his own.
2 and 3 Superintendence of estate, investment, politics, intellectual pursuits,	To ideal of enjoyment and display.
3 Idleness,	To ideal of enjoyment.

III — PARALLEL DEVELOPMENT OF INSTITUTIONS RELATING TO SOCIAL ORGANIZATION

So much for the habits of common life according to which man obtains a livelihood, and subjugates and uses for his advantage the forces and phenomena of material nature, the ways in which he spends his time. We now turn to what are called more distinctly the social institutions. And first is that which is the foundation of social life, the family.

In early Rome, family life not only was, but was considered to be, of the highest importance. The Gens was the great power in society. In origin it was religious, an organization for the worship of tutelary deities, the gods of the hearth. But when the tribes arose, and more particularly when they were united, this character was lost, and the *curiae* became chiefly political. In the later days, the Name was highly valued ; the nobility cared a great deal for the reputation of the family in war, and strove to maintain its peculiar virtue everywhere ; but the family was not the political unit.

The Family— The Early Gens

From the primitive character of the Gens, we may judge the nature of marriage itself. While its essence lay simply in the consent of the two parties, it was the accomplishment of civil and religious obligations ; and by eating together the cake, the newly-wedded pair founded a fresh hearth in the Gens and a new family in the state. Naturally, with these obligations, celibacy was thought

Marriage

almost a crime. Divorce was carefully guarded, and was not allowed, except for reason, and then only after careful consultation of the Gens. Very stringent regulations were laid down in the XII Tables, and the divorce of Ruga, so late as 283, was the occasion of a great outcry.

As the marriage ceremony was religious, legal marriage was limited to those who were of Roman birth, *i. e.*, were members of some family. Others might live together, but their marriage was not recognized by the state, because they could not take part in the necessary religious rites.

Home Life

In the early family, the life seems to have been very much like that of what we to-day call a home. It may have been a little austere, but that was in the Roman blood. Marriages were happy and permanent, exposure of infants was not common and was only for what was considered good reason, and personally, the men and women lived lives of purity. The father had peculiar power over all the members of the family. Everything was his by right of *manus*; and it was by virtue of this right, and his position as a householder, that he had his separate citizenship. However, in the home, there seems to have been a feeling of equality; women ate with men and were present at their banquets. Although the father was the head of the family, and children and wife both belonged to him, yet the wife, howbeit lacking in authority, was his equal in dignity. As he had to do with the estate and with war, so she was in charge of the home and attended to all its belongings; he had his servants and she her maidens. And while, no doubt, the *patria potestas* was freely exercised in this early period, the life of the home seems, on the whole, to have been a life of happiness. Notwithstanding under the form of marriage by *manus* the wife was only a thing conveyed to her husband, she was highly reverenced. It was she who made the house what it was, and at her death the husband ceased to be a priest. It may also be noted that women were recognized as a part of the state, and could bear witness in the courts, which, however, they rarely did.

Changes in Marriage

All this was in accord with the early ideal of purity and morality, of national feeling, and paternal authority. But the workings of a new ideal, developments which did not here appear, or which, because of the scarcity of their appearance, pass unnoticed, made themselves manifest in the later republic. The first exceptions to the old rule of living were met with severity and great outcry, but such was not for long the case. The father's power remained as absolute as ever in the family. But the religious ceremony of marriage was gradually exchanged for the civil *coemptio*, and this in turn gave way to *usus*, by which the husband had legal authority over the wife only after a year of married life, without the passage of a *trinoctium* during which she had been absent from his house. Her property did not come with her to her husband, but she retained both it and her position in her own family. Marriage by *manus* was relegated to the priests, for whom alone, because of their office, it was a matter of necessity. Such a movement, of course, seriously impaired the stability of the family. Following the changing ideal, the tendency had been toward greater and greater laxity, and the price of this development was the permanence (and we may add, the happiness) of the family relation. The full fruit was borne in the evil society of the later republic and the early empire. The provision of *trinoctium* was then taken as a means of breaking troublesome bonds. Men, on the other hand, simply dismissed their wives without ceremony. The form of *usus* allowed man and woman to live together for a year without the woman's coming into the man's power; and at any time she could leave him, and it would have been nothing. And this gives, not the extreme possibilities of the law, but what was actually going on every day.

In another way of looking at this general matter, we may call it the emancipation of woman.[1] By the old law, a married woman was subject to her husband. She had no property of her own. The unmarried woman was subject to her nearest male *agnatus*, and had no right of management of her own property. But by various means, by mock marriages and by making use of the custom of *trinoctium*, women tried to get property into their own hands. Now by the Roman theory, only men were Roman citizens; consequently they alone should control the property. But so greatly had things changed from this, that in 169 it was felt necessary to exclude women from testamentary inheritance.

Or, the Emancipation of Woman

---

[1] So Mommsen, *ibid.*, ii: 476.

As time went on family jurisdiction over women became more and more antiquated. Their ideal, as that of the men, was gain and personal pleasure, and on account of the severity of their previous conditions, they seem to have been carried headlong to the other extreme.

<small>Morality of the Last Century before Christ</small>

Of the condition of things in Rome of the last century, in matters pertaining to the family, we do not need to say much here; for the state of affairs is too largely a matter of common knowledge to require a great deal of explanation. We get a hint of the situation from the odes of the poet Horace, and among writers of his day, he was above the average in purity. Some of his works are in their whole body unreadable; and it is only in excerpted editions that the works of many other Latin authors can be placed in the hands of readers to-day. The censors tried to stop this tendency, but were unable. Not alone as it appeared in the breaking up of family ties, but in all the life of Rome, the deadly virus was working. Augustus thought by his supreme power to check the alarming development. He promised rewards for the rearing of children, and made penalties for celibacy. But the bachelors perferred the flattery and adulation of their clients and of the captators; for they knew that if they should marry, these attentions would be no longer theirs. Horace at times sees and laments these things, and he sings warningly, "Our fathers were not as their fathers, nor are we as they, and our children shall be worse than ourselves."[1] But he received no more attention. The vices of Rome and the awful wickedness, not only of her nobility but of her whole population, demand our assent to the melancholy statement, "Rome fell because she had lost the old Aryan idea of the family."[2] A different, a new ideal was, as we have seen, the actuating idea of Roman society.

CAUSALITY.	THE FAMILY
1 Ceremony of *manus*, obligation and permanence of marriage, . .	Correspond to ideal of citizen as member of family.
Woman's dignity, ...	To place of family in ideal of state. Also to ideal of virtuous living.
Patria potestas,	To ideal of citizen as head of family.

[1] Horace: Odes, Book iii; ode 6.
[2] Thwing: The Family.

1c *Coemptio*,	Due to ideal of state aggrandizement which turned inward as well as outward. To incipient decay of ideal of virtuous living(?).
Emancipation of woman,	To growing ideal of personal gain and individual enjoyment.
Woman remaining a member of her own family, . . .	Due to ideal of family and personal aggrandizement.
Valuing and maintenance of Name,	Due to same.
2 and 3 *Usus, trinoctium*, laxity growing, ...	Due to gradually growing ideal of enjoyment and personal gratification.
Celibates (captators *et al.*), . .	Due to same, with something of display.
Immoral literature, . . .	Due to ideal of personal, sensual gratification and pleasure.

The beginnings of Rome we find, however, not in the family, but in the institutions of the state. To be sure, there is about the whole story the glamour and unreality of myth; yet whether we consider it as essentially true, or as framed in after years to account for certain necessary and probable events, the effect on our considerations will be little. In either case, it exhibits the prevailing temper of the early Romans. *The State*

Here are the bare facts. The first care of the infant state was for its political institutions; of these the projector was Romulus. Numa followed with the institutions of religion. Tullus Hostilius brought the Albans to Rome, the origin of the plebeian order, so in a sense founding the great social institution. And Ancus Marcius, devising the *fetiales*, laid down the primitive regulations of inter-tribal, or inter-national, relations. The affairs of the next reign bear more the appearance of historic truth. Tarquinius Priscus, perhaps the representative of an Etruscan conquest, led in great material progress, which he very likely copied from the surrounding nations. Servius Tullius gave to Rome a new military organization, that of the centuries, on the basis of property. He also divided all the people without respect to rank or property into local tribes, whose duties were to fix property taxes and to provide for military levies. Tarquinius Superbus made himself odious to the Roman people, and is chiefly noted for his expulsion; upon which event, the curies selected two prætors from among their number to be the twin executives of Rome. *The Kingdom*

We may notice, in the first place, about this history, that the early kings held office, not by any inherent right, but by the gift of the people. Romulus was simply a superior member of the Ramnes (and before that, the leader of a robber band); and Numa was put forward to stand for the Tities. On the contrary, the last three kings seem to have assumed a right to themselves. According to the story, the elder Tarquin, as regent, usurped the power of the two sons of Ancus Marcius. Upon the assassination of Tarquin by the sons of Ancus, Servius Tullius, through the stratagem of Tanaquil, was proclaimed king. And the haughty Tarquin gained his place by the crime of his brother's wife.

<small>Seat of Authority</small>

The expulsion of the kings, therefore, was not of the nature of a primary revolution. The guilty deed of Sextus was but the occasion for the assertion by the people of the rights which they felt were theirs by inheritance, and which had been held in abeyance by the last three kings. By the casting off of the yoke of oppression, the power was simply returned to those who had given it, by them to be meted out to worthy leaders, who by their annual deposition should continually bear witness to the popular residence of political authority.

The division, therefore, of the early history of the Roman people at the expulsion of the kings is rather on the surface. That answers, instead, to the usurpation of the elder Tarquin, and it is eleven years after that there appears a real boundary line. *Populus Romanus* meant only those who, being of Roman birth or adoption, were numbered in some *curia*. Outside these, there had grown up a large plebeian population about the Alban nucleus. Excluded from political privileges and trodden down by the patricians, at once their superiors and their heavy creditors, in 494 they finally made a determined stand upon *Mons Sacer*. In vain did the patricians' representatives try to persuade them to return to the city. They would not do so, until their demands were met. And so it came about that all existing debts were canceled; all debtors in bondage were restored to freedom; the plebeians were given two plebeian ædiles, and were granted two tribunes of the plebs, who should have the care of plebeian interests and to whom the plebeians might appeal from the decision of any magistrate. This marks a dividing

<small>The Republic, 494-286 B. C. — True Division at 494 not 505</small>

line in early Roman history. The common people had become sufficiently conscious, not of their ill treatment, but of their rights as men, to demand them at the hands of the patricians. And this view is further supported by the statement of the historian that those who retired to the Sacred Mount were orderly in their behavior, and were not an unorganized mob, or a band of plunderers.

In 286, the long struggle was finally ended, so far as patrician and plebeian contestants were concerned, by the Hortensian Law. By this it was enacted that the *plebiscita*, of themselves and without the necessity of any exterior sanction, should be binding on all the Quirites.

To go over this struggle in detail would be tedious and not to our purpose. We may simply call up its main points: The Decemvirate in 451, whose appointment was the culmination of a ten years' effort on the part of the plebs; the second secession to *Mons Sacer*, following the matter of Virginia, and the subsequent passage of the Valerian and Horatian laws; the secession to the Janiculum in 445, which secured the right of inter-marriage of plebeians with patricians; the Licinian Rogations in 367, the outcome of another long battle on the part of the tribunes; in 338, the Publillian laws; in 300, the *Lex Ogulnia*, which gave to the plebeians a place in the religious hierarchy; and in 286, the *Lex Hortensia*. Soon after the Licinian Rogations, there seems to have been a very decided movement on the part of the plebs, and many of the offices were occupied by them. The complete organization of the army, giving to each citizen some place, and the provision by which the spoil of battle was equally distributed, afforded them much encouragement and made them more devoted to the state. In the later part of this period, the patricians became much reduced in numbers and were compelled to seek outside aid. So that the division finally was not plebeians against patricians, but the popular party, consisting of the main body of the plebs, against the patricians and their allies, the lowest freemen, the four city tribes.

Main Facts of the Plebeian Struggle

It is interesting to note the provisions upon which emphasis was placed by their reiteration, in the measures passed for the benefit of the plebs. Taking them in the order in which they appeared in

Contested Points

legislation, the right of appeal of every citizen was three times affirmed (494, 449 (2)); three laws related to indebtedness (494, 367, 323), the last abolishing imprisonment for debt; quite a number, at least four (486, 450, 392, 367), dealt with agrarian matters; five had to do with the decrees of the Comitia Tributa (449 (2), 339, 286 (2)), the control of the senate and the curies being by the last forever done away; three (445, 367, 300), concerned the religious rights of the plebs.

Our most important question, however, is as to the temper of this political period. It is a feature, as we might expect from the national character of the ideal, that the bone of contention was the state. Each man fought and worked for citizenship and for a share in the government, whether large, as that of the patricians, or small, as that sought by the plebeians. It was a period of activity and great originality in the field of politics. Rome was altogether a "live" community. It is worth noting, too, that although the plebs were fighting for their rights, and although each law which came into being was the idea or the compulsory gift of the patricians, every one was ready for patriotic endeavor. Indeed, it was a common ruse of the nobility to lead out the legions to war, with or without pretext, in order to overcome the growing discontent.

Temper of the People

There is one political custom of this period which seems to show us the Republic herself sowing the seeds of her future troubles, in the cultivation of a dangerous ideal. Before the annual elections, each citizen who sought office was compelled to candidate. Assuming the white toga, he must enter the Forum, and there solicit the votes of his fellow-citizens by exhibiting his honorable scars and by telling what he would accomplish if elected. Turbulent as Roman elections usually were, the cultivation of this self-seeking spirit brooked for her things far worse than the tumult of her citizens. Sometime, what was now only the expression of popular feeling would be organized to forward the plans of personal ambition.

Unfavorable Signs

Over the latter part of this epoch, the new aristocracy began to form. In its growth it has been compared to that of a crust of ice upon the water, increasing slowly but surely in thickness and in strength.

The dominant cry of the following years was, Rome against the world. Externally they formed an age of conquest ; internally they were marked by con- *The Republic,* solidation and incipient demoralization, the Party *286¹-146 — Social Aristocracy* of Reform, and the beginning of the breaking up. The aristocracy, as we have just said, was not destroyed, but only re-organized. So early as 310, there was a very sharp distinction between curule and non-curule members of the senate. To the former alone was the right of debate allowed, although the latter sat in large numbers. For some time the nobility were a class honorably distinguished, and upheld by the high offices ; but gradually, after the second Punic war, they declined into "an order of lords, filling up their ranks by hereditary succession and exercising collegiate misrule." In 190 the senate was, as characterized by Mommsen, " made up of coteries of men striving for family aggrandizement." But meanwhile, they had not left themselves without support. The censorship was, from its very inception, a staff for the patricians; the senate with its curule privileges was another prop ; and lastly, the Equites had been converted into an aristocratic corps, throwing to the winds the doctrine of military equality, and making an arm of the service which, from the military point of view, was not altogether strong, but affording much strength to the aristocratic position by its control of the Comitia Centuriata. In illustration of the power of the Comitia, it is probably true that Manius Curius, elected in 274, was the last consul who did not belong to the social aristocracy. Nevertheless, the supremacy on the part of the nobility was largely a piece of assumption. There is no doubt that the real power was in the hands of the people, if they had only cared or dared to use it. But so much inured were they to the old customs that they discouraged radical changes. They even, for instance, refused to accept a bill which transferred the election of pontiffs from the curies to the tribes.

Some censors, however, did not hesitate to exercise their official authority with rigor, when there was occasion for it. During the first Punic war *Party of Reform* (262–240), thirteen senators and forty knights

---

[1] The date 286 is of course not absolute. It only seems, on the whole, to be the most suitable. So 146 is entirely arbitrary ; but we justify it by the simultaneous conquest of Carthage and Greece.

were degraded because of their lukewarmness in the service of the republic. 234 and 149, the limits of the life of the elder Cato, may be taken as the dates of the Reform Party, of which he was the great leader. It represents the opposition of the middle class of Rome, her back-bone, to the "Hellenic-cosmopolite nobility." When Cato presented himself as a candidate for the censorship, it was with the avowed purpose of purifying the senate and the nobility. To this service he was chosen by the votes of the Reform Party; and their persistence is shown by the fact that, though Cato was forty several times accused by the nobility, he was each time acquitted by the votes of these supporters.

It is natural that the number of police regulations and of sumptuary laws at this time should be unusual. For a while they undoubtedly checked the political and moral decay. But they lacked permanent effect, because their promoters acted on the defensive rather than the offensive, and were apparently without a definite plan or a thorough understanding of the trouble. The party was wealthy in good citizens but it had no great statesmen.

Loss of Unity and of Political Honesty

In the latter part of this period, the burden of the Roman wars was thrown increasingly on the Latin and Italian allies. The unity on the basis of republican freedom which marked the short epoch of the Samnite wars was breaking up before the encroachments of the senate. The city rabble and their accordant demagogues were a growing political force. Of the bright days of Rome, Polybius said that "nothing is held more base (by her citizens) than to be corrupted by gifts, or to covet an increase of wealth by means that are unjust." In 170, she had an honorable reputation for fair dealing and for honesty in the administration of her dependencies: but this did not long continue. And the same change was soon marked at home as well.

Later Republic. 146-29 B. C.— Character of Government

It would not be correct to think that we have now come to the era of Rome's degradation; we have merely approached its brink. And the period down to the foundation of the empire only finds it well established. There was an increasing tendency not to have any interest in or connection with the affairs of the state. The shallows, however, are bad enough. The struggle in these later times was that of power and wealth against the people. The history of the government is the history of the rise and fall of individuals. As Niebuhr says, "With the elder Gracchus, we come to the period where each character presents a separate psychological problem." The two Gracchi, Marius and Sulla, Crassus, Pompey, and Cæsar, each with more or less thought for the welfare of the people, waged or excited civil war. The character of the legislation shows that things had changed. *Leges Frumentarii* were common, the expression of a most short-sighted policy, but answering, however, to the ideal in which personal interests had taken precedence of the welfare of Rome. Internally, there was no controlling power in the state. Formerly men had been restrained by the personal scrutiny of magistrates and of their fellow-citizens, but Rome had grown too large for this — "a multitudinous monarch without the capacity for vigilance."

So far as foreign policy was concerned, there was but one; the empire for use rather than for administration. There was no idea of provincial representation. Rome simply tried to stretch her city government to fit an empire, and of course she was destined to fail. Either the provinces must be brought up to her level, or she must sink to theirs; the latter was what took place. Foreign Policy

In the matter of revenues, all was not true and upright. Polybius says that there was "hardly a man of means in Rome who had not been concerned, as an avowed or silent partner, in the leasing of the public revenues." And again, "In general, artifice so much prevails that it is now become the chief study of men to deceive each other, both in the administration of civil affairs and in the conduct of war."[1] The condition in the provinces may be judged from the conduct of Licinius in Greece, who turned everything to his own account, even selling furloughs to the soldiers, and from the notable case of Verres. Malfeasance

Add to this the proscriptions, all too frequent in the later days of the republic, the daily uncertainty of private as well as public life and fortune, the fact that only a few could by any possibility rule, and behind these, the very individual nature of Further Causes and Manner of Re-adjustment

---

[1] Polybius: History, Book xiii; extract 1.

the ideal, and it is no wonder that the general desire was for peace and good government at any cost, and the great fear, that of another civil war. Many successes, and particularly that of Pompey in quelling the pirates, had strengthened the popular confidence in the dictatorship, so that it was gladly accorded to Cæsar, and in turn to Octavian, as a secure form of public administration. Under this arrangement, government soon became more equitable; centralization and order were substituted for anarchy. But at the same time, there was loss of liberty. Gradually Augustus drew to himself all the powers of the different magistrates. The forms of popular legislation ceased to be observed. The emperor formed about himself a cabinet. There grew up a new official organization. The imperial government was a unity, but on the basis of servitude; and the authority which had been accorded the popular leaders was soon demanded by an emperor.

Summaries of Political Development By a couple of summaries, we may, perhaps, make more clear the parallelism of this development in politics to the development of the moral ideal. The progress, we should bear in mind, was from a strong national morality and pride to a predominant desire for individual gratification and power. Originally, the ideal Roman was, in a single word, a patriot. By insensible degrees, he became the man of family and personal reputation, and then the man of pleasure.

First, as to the ground of political authority: In the senate, the basis of membership was, at the beginning, age; the old men were entrusted with the affairs of the state. But as the plebeian element grew, this qualification was lost sight of in the emphasis placed on noble birth. This by a gradual process was superseded by the criterion of necessary wealth, and the senatorial rights were tacitly confined to the social aristocracy, till finally the name "senator" became a synonym for social position and prestige and the senate little more than the creature of the emperor. In the comitial organization, the curies respected both birth and age. The centuries, to which the government was handed over, were based upon wealth, though, in their organization, the *seniores* had a majority over the *juniores;* and the Equites, who held the preponderance of power, came to be, as a class, men of noble blood. In the Comitia

Tributa, the source of authority was power. Of course, along with these requirements, there was a certain amount of ability necessary for leadership.

Again, according to the main object of government: The very early history deals with the framing of political forms ; but after that, we find the three branches of government occupied somewhat in this way :

DEPARTMENTS	REPUBLIC			TRANSITION	EMPIRE
	To 494.	494–286.	286–146.	146–29.	29–
Executive, . . .	Defence.	Defence.	Conquest.	Conquest and civil war.	Security.
Judiciary, . . .	Justice to Romans.	Justice to citizens.	And also to aliens.	To same and fluctuating.	To all— within limits.
Legislative, . .	General welfare.	And class interests.	Class interests.	Popular desires and individual will.	Will of emperor.

CAUSALITY. THE STATE

(Ideals which dominate in later periods are traceable far back; in some cases it is difficult to speak exactly regarding causality).

1 Formation of the state ;
   Politically, . . .   Corresponds to ideal of man as citizen (and head of family).
   Religiously,   To ideal of man as head of family, what must have been originally a family institution being made a part of the state.
   Socially, orders of patricians and plebeians, . . .   Correspond to ideal of citizen as member of a family.
   Internationally, . . .   To ideal of keeping faith(?).
   Power resident in people, . .   To ideal of man as citizen.
   Senate and curies by noble birth, .   To place of family in ideal.
1b Plebeian struggles, ...   Due to ideal of man as citizen, working in those who were not citizens.
   Devotion to state, . . .   To patriotic ideal.
   Struggle on part of patricians,   In part, to ideal of man as member of family; also same; also ideal of later times can be noticed.
   New aristocracy,   To beginning of ideal of personal aggrandizement.
   Control and membership in centuries,   To ideal of man as citizen; as a member of family; also sign of personal aggrandizement.
1c Consolidation, . .   Due to ideal of state aggrandizement.
   Party of Reform, . .   To same; devotion to state.
   Social aristocracy, . .   To ideal of honorable living and to growing ideal of personal gain.
   Growing city rabble and demagogues, loss of unity and honesty, .   To ideal of personal gain and aggrandizement now growing.

1*c* and 2 Senate based on wealth, Comitia Tributa; *power* the power,	To last, and that of honorable living. To ideal of personal aggrandizement.
2 Rise and fall of individuals,	Due to ideal of personal aggrandizement.
Rule of few, proscriptions, loss of state vigilance and power, little real citizenship, *Leges Frumentarii*, empire for use,	To ideal of personal gain.
Malfeasance, allowance, of dictatorship,	To same, and growing ideal of personal gratification.
3 Empire, loss of liberty, senate creature of the emperor,	To ideal of personal gratification.

Religion — Its Foundation

In the foundation of religion at Rome, there are three points in particular which claim attention. Religion had its first expression, not in the stirring songs of some gifted Homer, nor in the inspired utterances of ascetic prophets, but in the national policy of Numa, the king; religion was introduced by a king who was of Sabine, rather than Roman origin; although most closely connected with the state, religion was not its basis, but rather was superimposed upon it.

Its Character

With the early Romans the state was everything, and so the religion was a state religion. During the kingdom, the king was also the high pontiff of the nation. He had as his coadjutors the sacerdotal orders of pontiffs and augurs, the former to make sacrifices, and the latter to superintend the omens. The gods were thought of by the people as the prototypes of human virtues, and as the rulers of human affairs, but the emphasis was placed on this latter and the former practically disappeared quite early. The desire, consequently, was to obtain from these sovereigns of the earth advice, and a definite Yes or No, as to the execution and the success or failure of the projects of men. From the space which was marked off (*templum*) for the especial purpose, the augur would observe the flight of birds, at the sacrificial altar he would examine the entrails of the victim, and from these he claimed to be able, by certain secret, but infallible signs, to read the answer of the gods. It was but natural, since the gods were conceived as omnipotent rulers, that men should seek to gain their favor by propitiatory offerings, and this is the distinctive character of the gifts of votaries. Whether sacrifice was offered or a temple was vowed, each was in return for, or in expectation of, an equivalent return from the divinity. The dealings with the gods were strictly mercantile, and the oath made to them was on the same level as that to one's neighbor. The supernatural element was present in this religion only in the form of superstition; in general it was cold and prosaic, utterly different from the warm anthropomorphism of the Greek mythology, but thoroughly agreeing with the Roman sternness and austerity.

The power of the sacerdotal class, not only the sole interpreters of the omens, but also the guardians of the sacred books, was very great. The whole state was practically subject to them. When the title *rex* for a political sovereign was forever put away, as still retained in *rex sacrorum*, it was expressive of the seat of highest control. Religion was in theory founded on and supported by political institutions, but for a long time, as a matter of fact, it controlled national affairs. For example, it was compulsory upon public officials to consult the auspices before attempting any public work. And the priests were able to enforce their directions, not only by the weight of religious sanction or disapproval, but also by excommunication, both religious and political, which it was in their power to proclaim and to execute. Again, by the custom of *dies fasti* and *nefasti*, they controlled the legal affairs of all individuals. On one of the holy days, there could be no litigation or meeting of the Comitia. And since many of the dates were uncertain, and they were never published in advance, no one could tell, till he came to the city, what the chances for action that day would be. Power of the Priesthood

The great power thus placed in the hands of a few, by the very fact of its greatness, brought with it great temptations. The religion, limited in its range to those who could unite in the worship of some *curia*, was essentially a patrician institution, and when the struggle had commenced between the orders, the nobility did not hesitate to use it for their own ends. In not a long time, the influence of religion — which, we should bear in mind, rested on the authority of human laws and the efficacy of human institutions — was used, not to make men better, however much (or little) that may have been its object previously, but to render them more powerful. We may judge, then, that the *Lex Ogulnia*, by which one-half the pontiffs and augurs Corruption for Political Purposes were secured to the plebeians, was an enactment of no little importance.

But we must also notice that from this time the power of the priesthood began to wane. Even much as they valued the sacerdotal offices, the plebs cared more to be tribunes than to be pontiffs, for the Roman spirit was first civil and military and then religious. On the other hand, the lack of any object for which they might exercise religious control, and the absence of unbridled sway in religious affairs, caused the patricians to become lukewarm and indifferent. So when the plebs became priests, the power of the priesthood began to grow less; the office had been widened only to work its ultimate destruction.

Its Decay

What was true in the priestly orders was still more the case in the national religious life (if we may use such an expression). Even between the Punic wars, the state religion was tottering, and when Ennius declared about 200 B. C., "No doubt, I believe the gods exist, but they scarcely trouble themselves about the world," we are told by Cicero that many applauded.[1] In the time of Cato, the images of the gods were used by the wealthy as articles of furniture, as statuary for the adornment of their houses.

But the development which seems from this aspect only the loss of the old religion, in another embodies the extension of religious sentiment. Among other things, it had been the business of the priests to see to it, not only that aliens were excluded from Roman worship, but that Romans did not worship foreign deities, *i. e.*, those not permitted by law. So, when we see a temple reared to Castor and Pollux, it is by the state, for aid given the Roman arms in the battle of Lake Regillus; Apollo is adopted by the state during the Decemvirate; in 264, the worship of Cybele is introduced, likewise by the state; and later, it is the state that sends an expedition to import the god Aesculapius. It may be noted in passing, that each of these foreign worships was brought in under the pressure of exceptional circumstances (not, we should think, to create priesthoods for the plebeians).[2] But the significant thing is, that these

Introduction of Oriental Religions — By the State

---

[1] Cicero: De Divinitate, ii: 50.
[2] As Guhl and Koner: The Life of the Greeks and Romans, p. 304.

alien deities were admitted by the state as such, and that their admission was dependent, ultimately, upon the action of the state.

In 186, the discovery of the Bacchanalian revels shocked the better moral sense of the community. But from the religious point of view, the offence was quite as serious, for the worship of Bacchus had been introduced without the consent or approval of the state. *By Individuals*
The reappearance of these orgies in 180, in spite of the severe punishment meted out only six years before to so great a number as 7,000 guilty persons, shows that neither in its immorality nor in its irreligion was it a spasmodic outburst. It, and the previous introductions, perhaps more especially that of the worship of Cybele, were symptoms in religion of the growth of an individualistic ideal, now fast approaching the point where it would be beyond restraint.

These newly introduced Oriental religions possessed a warmth which was at the opposite extreme from early Roman institutions. They appealed particularly to the passions, and it was in the glorification of these that the personal ideal found its field. *Their Power* The natural evolution here brought about skepticism among thinking men, and turned them either, in despair, into the popular current, or toward Oriental mysticism, or left them wandering in the obscure by-ways of Stoic casuistry.

We find the rites of the old religion observed far into the empire. But, fortunately or unfortunately, religion and religious observances are two different things. Rome required the gods for the purposes of the state, long after men had ceased *Use of the Old Religion* to believe in them. The position taken by her statesmen was that religion was a valuable instrument of government, especially among the lower classes. Polybius gives this as the common view, in his opinion. Cicero and Varro thought religious restraints essential to the public welfare and safety. And public policy decreed that in the government of the provinces, the religions of the various peoples should not be molested. "*Cujus regio, ejus religio.*"

It may be an occasion for surprise, that Stoicism did not ex-

Influence of Stoicism

ert a stronger influence among the Romans in general. With some, it was a powerful factor; Cato and Cicero are only two examples, among a great number. But it would seem that its effect upon the large majority was not so much positive, furnishing them with a new belief, as it was reactionary, driving them further away from the old divinities. Roman religion, as we have already noted, offered but very slight nourishment for the religious emotions. There was, and had been — for the Romans were men — a gradually growing, and now most intense desire for a positive religious belief. Stoicism with its cold intellectuality and its dry dialectic was not suited at all to quench this thirst. Instead, it only made its assuaging the more imperative. A concurrence of political and commercial conditions opened the way in congenial Oriental directions, and there the thirsting religious nature, in one cup and another which it quaffed to the dregs, caught at any rate the flavor of that nectar which it was so fervidly seeking.

CAUSALITY.	RELIGION
(Ideal runs back further here; seems to make itself manifest most easily in religion, and yet to linger there as well.)	
1 First expression in political policy, superimposed on state,	Corresponding to ideal of man as citizen and to place of state in ideal.
King was *pontifex*, new divinities introduced by state, vows,	To ideal of keeping faith, from idea of gods as great men.
1*b* Patrician priesthood,	Due to ideal of man as member of family.
Corruption for political purposes,	To ideal, now manifested among patricians, of family aggrandizement.
Lex Ogulnia,	To ideal of personal gain; also devotion to the state in plebs.
1*c* Decay of priesthood,	Due to ideal of family and personal aggrandizement.
Indifference to religion,	To ideal of personal gain.
Introduction of Oriental religions by individuals,	To ideal of personal gain; and sensual gratification.
Roman religion an instrument of government among lower classes,	To ideal of state, and later of family and personal aggrandizement.
2 Strength of Oriental religions, Lack of influence of Stoicism to the same.	To ideal of sensual gratification and of pleasure.

Society — Classes

In noting the development of society itself, we look, first, at social divisions. There were three classes in early Rome, patricians and clients, who were freemen, and slaves. Clients were either aliens, who were regarded only for their occupations, or plebeians. The distinction between these latter and the patricians we have already viewed in its political aspect. It was even more harsh from the point of view of social customs. The patricians based their superiority on birth, which secured to them all their rights. Plebeians, if admitted by adoption to any *curia*, obtained this only as a privilege. They were essentially conquered men. They had no rights. Patricians exacted from them services in war, submission in peace, and bondage in their poverty. And not only were they a subject class; they were a separate caste, worshiping by different religious rites, and without the privilege of intermarriage with their superiors, indeed, without the legal ability of contracting formal marriage all. If any further sign of this class difference is needed, we find it in the separate places in which public meetings were held. The patricians assembled in the Comitium, with its stately buildings and majestic associations, the plebeians in the Forum, with its noise and rush of busy trade.

As the years passed by, there was a marked degeneration in the system of clientage. Disappearing with the decay of the old patricians and the increasing rights of the plebs, the relation was afterward resurrected on a new basis. The old dependency was widened, till the clientage of one man included a whole town, and in the later times, the relation subsisted between senators and provincial cities, that is, the senators represented them at Rome. Meantime a new clientage sprang up at Rome. In it the clients lacked not only rank but wealth. They hung upon their patrons even for their daily bread, and saw nothing disgraceful in their pursuit. On the other hand, their patrons were equally delighted by their presence; and they did not feed the crowd without getting something in return. The larger the retinue of clients that escorted one to the Forum in the morning, the greater man was he. <small>Change in Clientage</small>

We do not find the aristocratic distinction wiped out at any time; it is characteristic of Roman history. But we do find its basis altering. In the early times, the ground of nobility was birth. But as we read along, about 275 we are conscious of a change. The old patricians were soon so scant in numbers that not they, but the better class of plebeians formed the nobility; <small>Later Society — Basis of Nobility</small>

and from this there soon developed the social aristocracy, based on wealth and political standing. There was a differentiation, too, in the kinds of greatness, and moneyed superiority was quite as decided as political or military.

In the early days, all had belonged, in a sense, to the middle class. But in later times, we have, on the one hand, the *optimates* with their immense fortunes, and on the other, the city rabble; there was no middle class. An almost incredible number were fed at the public expense. In the year 70 B.C., it was one-third of the whole population.[1] Cæsar found 320,000, three-fourths of the people, on the rolls of public succor, and limited the number to 150,000, while Augustus is said to have *reduced* the paupers to 200,000. The saddest thing about this class division is, not simply that there were so many beggars and hangers-on, and that their condition was what it was, but that the rich were content that it should be so; they would do nothing to keep the lower classes from sure ruin. Social distinctions, as well as those other institutions which we have traced, followed the rudder of desire for personal power and enjoyment.

The Rabble

CAUSALITY.	CLASSES
1 Patricians and clients,	Corresponds to ideal of citizen as member (head) of family.
1*b* Different places of meeting of patricians and plebeians,	Due to same — essentialness of family ties to ideal of full citizenship.
Only middle class,	To ideal of citizenship still continuing.
1*c* Provincial clientage,	To ideal of personal aggrandizement.
2 Social aristocracy,	To ideal of family and personal aggrandizement.
Moneyed superiority,	To ideal of personal aggrandizement.
2 and 3 *Optimates* and city rabble; no middle class,	To ideal of personal gain and pleasure.

The same ideal appears in the facts of slavery. On the face of things, the greatest development at Rome was in the number of slaves. In the early days, slaves were few, for the captives taken in war were not many, and the only other ways of increase were the rearing of slave children and the enslaving of insolvent creditors — only aliens or plebeians, however, for no Roman citizen might serve another. The foreign conquests were the oc-

Slavery — Number of Slaves

---

[1] Brace: Gesta Christi, pp. 97, 98.

casion of a large increase in the number of captives. From all over the world they poured into Rome, and were sold at prices cheap enough for anyone. So it came about that the duties of the house and the estate were gradually given over to slaves; each little office had its bearer. From the servant who cleaned the marbles to the cook and the *nomenclator*, they were a great army in the houses of the aristocracy. So large was the number of slaves in Rome, that, when a special dress for them was proposed in the Senate, the project was finally dropped for fear of an uprising, should they learn their numbers.

In the early days, the slave was to some extent a member of the family. He ate his meals at the family table; he was somewhat acquainted with his master. But increasing numbers made this impossible. Instead of the family meal, each slave received a *peculium*, on which he might live and save what he could. He saw his master when he was purchased in the slave market; but he rarely came in contact with him, unless he held a responsible position in the household. This increase in numbers, and the accompanying separation from the family, fostered the idea that a slave was merely a thing, and so led to harsh and cruel treatment. In early Rome the lot of the slave had been tolerable, but the Servile Wars and the revolt of Spartacus show that it was not so in the later days. It was a law of the XII Tables that the plough, the beasts of burden, and the slaves should not work on holidays, of which there were about forty-five in the year. But Cato advised that slaves be, on those days, set at kinds of work which were not expressly forbidden, while the plough and the oxen rested; for "a slave must either work or sleep." Add to this the fearful punishments (to the cruelty of which masters were singularly impenetrable) and the tortures which were inflicted for trivial mishaps, *e. g.*, the case of the slave whom Pollio ordered thrown to the lampreys, and it is little wonder that a proverb ran, "So many slaves, so many foes."

<small>Condition</small>

Again, if we may judge at all by general conditions, the slaves were, in the early times, of good stock and of some character. But the importations of the Eastern conquests were steeped in Oriental vices. In the time of Cæsar the whole slave class was thoroughly

<small>Character</small>

demoralized and degraded. And, most unfortunately, by reason of this very fact, they were the more able to furnish their masters, in many an instance, with such amusements as they most desired.

CAUSALITY.	SLAVERY
1 Only captives, slave children, and alien or pleb debtors,	Corresponding to patriotic ideal.
Place for slave in family,	To ideal of man which, while denying slaves certain privileges, still saw in them the remainder of manhood. Largely circumstances.
1c and 2 Importation of slaves,	Due to ideal of state aggrandizement.
Increase in numbers,	To ideal of honorable living and personal aggrandizement.
Slave a thing,	Due to ideal of personal aggrandizement, as well as numbers.
2 and 3 Immense number,	To ideal of personal gain and display.
Harsh and cruel treatment,	To ideal of personal pleasure, selfish gratification.
Estate cared for by slaves,	To ideal enjoyment and luxury.
Acceptability of slaves of very low character,	To ideal of selfish and sensual gratification.

Amusements.— Early

If it is true that in their amusements people act more freely and unguardedly than at other times, then in their recreations we should see a most close correspondence to the development of the ideal. For the early Romans we may let Horace speak. "The husbandmen of early times, robust and easily contented, recreated themselves, when the harvest was gathered by feasts. With their slaves, children, and wives, they offered a hog to the earth, milk to Silvanus, and flowers and wine to the genius of the hearth." Such were the rural pleasures of these early men. King Tarquin the Elder erected for them a circus, and instituted athletic games. Music received but little attention; for highly as it was esteemed and earnestly as it was cultivated in later Rome, in these days musical ability, or any proficiency in music, was thought effeminate and degrading. And as for poetry, the Romans had no genius for that. In general, the probabilities would indicate for these games a display of strength and brute force, rather than of grace or of distinctive skill. The object, as in all amusements of Rome, early or late, was to entertain, not to instruct or elevate.

The innovation which worked woe for the circus was the gladiator. First seen in funeral games, he caught the popular fancy, and from that time he grew in popular favor. Different theories have been put forward to account for his introduction, and each of them accords with some characteristic of the ideal. For instance, man is in relation with the unknown on the basis of "for value received"; so the combatants were an offering to the Manes, who, by common belief, loved blood. Again, as the ideal called for activity and effort, men were not satisfied with representations, but wanted the real thing. So the drama had no hold on Rome. Comedy could endure, if it were realistic and sensual enough; but tragedy, only on the arena, where the bitter struggle for life or death was not painted but lived.

Introduction of the Gladiator

The desire for excitement, spurred on by almost daily exhibitions, at length demanded a stronger intoxicant, that the ideal of personal enjoyment might find satisfaction. The beasts appeared, fighting with one another, at first; but next, they were used to put an end to the lives of public offenders, or the gladiators were matched against them. In the early days of the empire, "To the beasts! To the beasts!" was a popular cry, and it foretold the death of many a faithful believer. This greed for pleasure and excitement, which was more fully gratified if there were the added charm of novelty, did not stop at cruelty of any degree. Scenes too horrible to relate were enacted in the circus. By the command of one emperor, human torches served to light his pleasure gardens. Another ordered two fully-equipped armies to take ship in the harbor, and there, encountering each other, to fight not a sham but a real battle, for the amusement of the populace. The great desire of this rabble was for bread and shows, nor did they blush at any immorality; in fact, this gave zest to all amusements, and especially to the presentations of the stage. Of Cato, it is related that, when he was censor, and this was previous to 200 B. C., he left the theater before the dancing girls appeared, in order that he might not be compelled to exercise his office, to the restraining of the enjoyment of the people. But someone has called him an "animated anachronism;" evidently he was in some things.

Later Shows

Two common forms of amusement were the Fescennine verses and the Atellane farces. Of the first Horace goes on from the quotation we have just made to say, " The fescennine license, springing from these festivals, poured out its rustic sarcasms in dialogue. At first it was only gay pastime, but this jesting ended by becoming spiteful, and assailing the most honorable families. Those whom this cruel tooth had wounded obtained the passage of a law which forbade, on pain of chastisement, any personal attack. The custom was changed for fear of the rod." Changed in expression, but not in nature. For scurrilous and low verses were what the mob, in after years, hugely enjoyed.

Fescennine Verses and Atellane Farces

The Atellane farces were introduced as a sort of religious rite. Participated in only by the sons of patricians, they by this fact long retained the odor of respectability, but not the rich perfume of their early purity.

But the mimes were what captured the popular heart in the way of theatrical representations. They were of Italic origin. The Greeks, too, derived them from Italy; but with them, dialogue occupied the principal place. With the Romans, this was of minor importance. The main thing was gesture and mimicry, the actors relying upon suggestion for their effect on people's minds. At first, these exhibitions were probably healthy, and a real amusement. But in the later days, they waxed more and more wanton, for the desires of the common heart and the strings upon which these Alituri played were one.

Mimes

Similar is the change that came over Roman feasts. In early times, these were not heavy; and after the repast, the recitations of the guests, interspersed with singing, formed the evening's entertainment. But not so in Cicero's time. The banquets of even the pontiffs and the Salii were proverbial for their prodigality. Feasts were midnight revels, after the Oriental fashion, with perhaps an intermission for exercise and bathing; and by the same standard, the chief amusements were voluptuous music and the exhibitions of Asiatic dancing girls. So, too, no merrymaking had formerly been thought complete, in which there was no display of patriotic feeling; but the Roman of the civil wars

Feasting

and the empire let politics and the emperor alone, either by choice, because he was self-centered and cared for none of these things, or by that worldly prudence which made one wary of eaves-dropping informers. Thus did the ideal value before all other things the interests of self.

An incident of the year 167 is illustrative of the popular feeling on the matter of amusements. Coming at the early part of the foreign growth, it may also stand for what follows. At some triumphal games of that year, certain Greek flute-players appeared; but it was evident that they did not please the multitude. Finally they were ordered to throw down their flutes and box; whereat the crowd greatly applauded.

<small>Illustration of the Popular Feeling</small>

Dice-throwing, too, had its share of patronage; but it was not limited to an after-dinner amusement. The Romans were always gamblers, more or less; but in the time of Augustus, this had become a veritable mania. We consider Monte Carlo a blot on society to-day; but how many times worse it would be, if that small island were the capital, political and social, of the whole world. Yet such was Rome. Everybody gambled; gambling was one of the supports of Roman restaurants. Some of the wagers were enormous, and many fortunes were ruined by the habit. Augustus tried to prohibit games of chance by law; there was a special provision to prevent them at meal-times. But he could not stop gambling any more than increasing luxury or dying patriotism. They were the work, all of them, of one ideal. And the contagion was even spread by succeeding emperors, who themselves overran the laws.

<small>Gambling</small>

The tendency of the ideal to display is manifest in the funeral ceremonies. In the early days, the body of the departed was borne out quietly at night and laid to rest, the relatives afterward joining in a funeral supper. Ostentation in these matters was very carefully guarded against in the XII Tables. But in the Rome of Caesar, the hour had moved forward into the late afternoon. First, the criers loudly proclaimed the funeral, and then the procession, issuing from the house, escorted the body through the streets to the Forum, and finally to the funeral pyre on the Appian Way. The richer the trappings and the

<small>Funeral Ceremonies</small>

grander the display the better. Even mimes were included in the procession, not only for the imitation of the actions of the deceased and his ancestors, but also for the amusement of the crowd. Games were offered to the public in the circus, and there were distributions of meat and corn. But the poor were borne out silently at night and buried in *puticuli* in the Campus Esquilinus.

In this consideration of social customs, we may include the change in wearing apparel. The national garb was the *toga*, and long was it worn with the reverence born of patriotic devotion. The first innovations were in the way of more complicated folding, then colors were used, and finally only the imperial edict could keep some from wearing purple of Tyrian dye. Others were tired of the garment altogether; it was uncomfortable and did not give enough chance for display. Augustus had to order the *toga* worn at court; in other places the *pallium* took its place. When we remember the position in the mind of the early Roman of everything which had to do with Rome, we can understand the significance of this action.

Disuse of the Toga

In Rome, as with us now-a-days, lounging was the common device by which time was whiled away. The difference is that the Romans were professional loungers; after the client had called for his *sportula*, and the *captator* had waited on the wealthy old bachelor, and the rabble has gone for their distribution of corn, the whole remainder of the day was spent in lounging about. For the loungers, the baths and the circus furnished opportunity. The latter, when not in use for the games, was the great resort of the common people, and it, rather than the Forum, became the place where they expressed their will. Likewise, it was characterized by their common amusements. It was here, for them, that the beasts devoured and the gladiators fought; and it was here that the *caveae* below the dens of the beasts hid from the light of day their nefarious traffic. Attend to Seneca's deliverance upon the times in which he lived, and so judge the tendencies of this excitement craving people. "Daily," he writes, "the appetite for sin increases, the sense of sin diminishes. Casting away all regard for right and justice, lust hurries whithersoever it will." (*De Ira*.)

Loungers and the Circus

CAUSALITY.   AMUSEMENTS AND OTHER CUSTOMS

1	Pastoral feasts, displays of strength, Toga,	Correspond to simple rural idea.
	Quiet funeral ceremonies; true mourning, apparently,	To citizen ideal. To citizen ideal, and place of family in ideal.
2 and 3	Gladiator,	Due to ideal of display; then of pleasure.
	Growing cruelty and shamelessness, degradation of Fescennine verses and Atellane farces, mimes very bad, feasts oriental in settings and amusements, circus and its customs,	Due to ideal of selfish, and more particularly, sensual, gratification.
	Nothing of patriotism at feasts,	To ideal of personal gain.
	Ostentatious funerals,	To ideal of display.
	Disuse of *toga*,	To ideal of personal pleasure.
	Gambling mania,	To ideal of gain and personal pleasure (excitement).
	Loungers,	To ideal of enjoyment.

IV — PARALLEL DEVELOPMENT OF INSTITUTIONS RELATING TO INDIVIDUAL CULTURE

Turning to the matter of education, we see there, also, quite a development. In ancient Rome the boy was in charge of his mother, but had no systematic education. In the early republic, however, we find private schools in charge of paid masters, for those who are somewhat older. About 225, the boys began to be put into the hands of tutors, usually slaves of foreign extraction. Cato did not believe in this, and it was esteemed worthy of note that he personally attended to the education of his son, even himself preparing some of his text-books. Still later, the Gracchi were peculiarly fortunate in having a mother capable and willing to train them. It was one secret of their true nobility. But these were uncommon instances. *[Education. Teachers]*

As to subjects, the schoolmaster taught reading, writing, and arithmetic (whence his title, *calculator* or *notarius*). For a long time this formed the body of instruction. Cicero, however, had to learn the XII Tables. In later times, early training was thought to be sort of an amusement. After the three fundamental studies, came the schools of the rhetoricians and grammarians. Here the boys were taught rhetoric and poetry, and had a taste of Greek philosophy. And at the age of 15 or 16, when the *toga virilis* was assumed, they were sent to Athens *[Subjects]* to be further educated in the schools of the philosophers. If a boy remained at home, he was free to attend the lectures of any instructor whom he might choose. Philosophy, however, was not the only thing that might be learned at Athens; and fortunate the youth who came back to Rome, even as pure and upright, as when he went away.

<small>General Character</small>

There was a general disapproval of sophistic teaching, when it made its appearance. The feeling was that it inculcated subversive doubt and taught things which were contrary to the traditions of Rome. Yet this teaching was what steadily gained ground. The early education was traditional. What the father had done the boy was to copy, and the power of the father was to be exercised in seeing that he so did. The later education was sophistic, and the youth, early turned out to pasture in the fields of learning, was allowed to gather what he would. So, correspondingly, the object of the early training was practical citizenship, including in its scope military exercises. The later equipment was for power and skill in managing men, or for refinement and culture. Athletics came in only incidentally, and as a matter of enjoyment. And on the whole, it was thought preferable to watch skilled wrestlers or contestants in any game, rather than to contest one's self. There was a great deal in the new education that was better than the old, but there was much that was worse. Horace seems to have felt this very deeply, when he says, "The young are brought up in idle, dissipated habits, and, instead of manly exercises, amuse themselves with the childish Greek sports; while their fathers," he adds, "are employed in making money by fraud."[1] And this is a truthful utterance regarding the education and habits of a notoriously evil city.

	CAUSALITY.	EDUCATION
1 Traditional, At home, Physical,	. . . .	Corresponds to place of family in ideal. To same. To ideal man as warrior, man of activity.
1b Both intellectual and physical, for citizenship,	. . . .	Due to place of state in ideal; ideal of man as citizen.

[1] Horace: Odes, iii: 24; 54.

1c Foreign tutors,	To beginning of family aggrandizement.
Cato and Cornelia, opposing, show the same in essence.	
2 and 3 Youth commonly sent to Athens,	To ideal of personal aggrandizement; and of pleasure.
Sophistic teaching, for skill in controlling men.	To ideal of personal gain.
For refinement and culture,	To ideal of enjoyment and display.
Watching others contest, instead of participating one's self,	To ideal of enjoyment, which had taken the place of that of activity.

For Summary, see following chart:

PERIOD	IDEAL	INSTITUTIONS			
		Subjugation of Nature			Social
		Material Welfare	Common Occupations	Family	State
Republican 753—146 B. C.	**Devotion to the State.** *Virtus et pietas.* Virtuous living.	Public buildings imposing. Tombs small and unornamented. Art sacerdotal. Dwellings mean. Fare frugal and life austere.	War and agriculture. Every man worked. War a duty—for defence—no standing army. Strength decided battles.	Religious. Politically important. *Gentes* formed *curiae*. Marriage by *manus;* permanent; one wife; limited to Romans. Divorce carefully guarded. Woman made the family. Father supreme. Home life austere but happy.	Kingdom. Kings hold office by gift of people. Last three kings usurpers, who are expelled. Republic. 494 .... Plebeian struggles. Tribunes of the plebs. State = the bone of contention. Gradually plebeians gain what they desire.
	286.........		Small farmers in Italy.		Popular party against patricians and four city tribes.
	Aggrandizement of the State. Honorable living.	Homes decorated. *Domi* of wealthy more and more ostentatious. Not so great contrast between public and private buildings.	Army for defence and conquest. Standing and paid. Legion.	Civil *coemptio.* "Emancipation of woman."	Consolidation. Incipient demoralization and Party of Reform. Social aristocracy gaining power. Loss of political honesty and of unity.
Transitional; Later Republic 146—29 B. C.	**Family and Personal Aggrandizement.** Personal gain. Money making.	New comforts; then extravagance.	War a business. Devotion to leaders. Reliance on cunning. Agriculture. Wholesale commerce. Politics. Study. Idleness.	Name highly valued, but *Gens* not the political unit. Family loses old permanence and happiness.	Power and wealth against the lower classes. Power usurped by senate. Provinces used, not administered. Burden of war and administration put on allies. Government = fall and rise of individuals.
			Italians give up estates and join city rabble.	*Usus. Trinoctium.* Great impurity.	*Leges Frumentarii.* Anarchy.
Empire 29—	**Enjoyment.** Selfish and sensual gratification; luxury; display.	Very rich and precious decorations of houses. Ornate tombs. Extravagance. Ostentation.	Idleness largely.	Family nearly destroyed.	Empire. Centralization and growth of order. Decline of popular legislation.

ROMAN IDEALS AND INSTITUTIONS—CHART

RELATING TO ORGANIZATION			INDIVIDUAL CULTURE	GROUND OF POLITICAL AUTHORITY	MAIN OBJECT OF GOVERNMENT
Religion	Social Customs		Education		
State religion on political basis. Cold; prosaic. Dealings with gods mercantile. Religion essentially patrician. Powerful priesthood; corrupted for political purposes.	*Caste*—Based on birth; patricians and clients; patricians and plebeians; all Romans born on a level. (Clientage decays.) *Slavery.*—Slaves few; captives; of good stock; lot tolerable; members of family. *Custom*—Toga national dress; pastoral amusements; athletic; strength rather than skill; feasts not heavy; accompanied by recitations and display of patriotic feeling. Fescennine verses, Atellane farces and mimes (they degenerate). Funerals quiet; introduction of gladiators at funeral games.		Early in charge of mother. Physical. Traditional not systematic. Private schools in charge of paid masters. Object: practical citizenship.	Senate: Age. Curies: Age and birth. Senate: Birth. Centuries: Wealth.	Executive: Defence. Judiciary: Justice to Romans. Legislative: General welfare. Executive: Defence. Judiciary: Justice to citizens. Legislative: Class interests.
Plebeians admitted to priesthood; its power wanes. Introduction of foreign divinities by state and by individuals.	Nobility based more and more on wealth and political position. Increase in number of slaves.		Foreign tutors. General disapproval of sophistic teaching.	Senate: Wealth and birth. Tribes: Power and ability.	Executive: Conquest. Judiciary: Justice to citizens and aliens. Legislative: Class interests.
Oriental worship. Skepticism, mysticism, Stoicism. Old religion retained as an instrument of government. Images of gods used for adornment of private houses.	*Caste*—Optimates and rabble. New clientage based on wealth. *Slavery*—Many slaves; cruel treatment; no connection with family; character vicious; Orientals largely. *Custom*—"Bread and shows;" great gladiatorial games and beasts; mimes very corrupt; gambling; feasts = midnight revels, accompanied by voluptuous music and dancing girls; no mention of state or government. Toga colored, then discarded. Funerals ostentatious.		Sophistic teaching. Schools of rhetoricians and grammarians. Object: skill and power, refinement and culture. Watching trained combatants preferable, on the whole, to contesting one's self.	Senate: Wealth and birth. Tribes and general: Power and wealth.	Executive: Conquest and civil war. Judiciary: Same and fluctuating. Legislative: Popular desires and individual will.
The same.			Similar.	Power.	Executive; Security. Judiciary: Justice to all within limits. Legislative: Will of emperor.

Chapter III

THE PARALLEL DEVELOPMENT OF IDEALS AND INSTITUTIONS IN THE ROMAN WORLD

Preliminary — Influence of Greece on Rome

When, a few pages back (p. 75), we turned from the development of the moral ideal of Rome to the parallel progress in institutions, we said that from the time of the empire, and even before, the distinctively Roman spirit was not present. Modification had occurred, chiefly owing to the influence of Greece. Before considering the Roman Empire, then, a word may not be out of place regarding the influence of Greece on Rome.

There are some who would here carry us back to the days of Numa. They would make him a Pythagorean, and Rome a state founded on Pythagorean principles. Of these men, however, Vergil is the most thorough, for he goes back to the beginning of things, and makes the original Romans Greeks. But coming out of this realm of fancy, it seems probable that Tarquin the Elder, when he instituted the games, may have done so according to Greek models. At all events, there was intercourse between the two peoples at the time of the Decemvirate, and that presupposes previous acquaintance. A committee of three was sent from Rome, at that time, to study the Athenian constitution; and one of the first apparent results of Greek influence was the introduction, upon their return, of the worship of Apollo.

After the Conquest

But the great power of Greece over Rome was manifested only after the conquest. Gentility, refined immorality, and intellectual penetration were Greece's most prominent characteristics. The process of Hellenization had already broken down Greek exclusion; indeed, her own population included many Orientals; and in this same Hellenizing process, conquered Greece in reality subdued victorious Rome. The intellectual and moral forces from 146 to the introduction of Christianity were increasingly Greek. For this there were several reasons. One was the great beauty and luxury of Eastern civilization, entirely foreign to Roman ways. Another was the rather uninventive temperament of the Romans, and their corresponding ability to apply to good advantage the inventions and discoveries of others. These, among other factors, brought it to pass that, in growing measure, Greek transformed Roman. The customs of the banquet were modeled after the Greek. The language of polite conversation was Greek, and a customary morning salutation in the Roman Forum was the Greek χαῖρε. The theater was taken bodily from the Greeks. The models in literary composition were Greek. The pedagogues were Greeks. And, to cap the climax, the great Roman university was Athens.

Two facts make this aping of Greece a matter of serious moment. One was the native coarseness of the Romans. Such sensitiveness and delicacy of refinement as marked the Greeks, they totally lacked. *Why a Serious Matter* Simulation or disguise of any kind was reproachfully alluded to as a Greek trait. The Greeks had an intellectual life, as distinguished from one which is physical. The Romans had only the latter, or, at least, the latter was primary. And thence, what were stains more or less unapparent on the Greek, became huge blots on the life of the Roman. The second was the Roman's lack of discrimination. He accepted every Greek custom as an integral part of Greek culture and refinement. So we find good and bad alike set up in Rome, and the warrant of "Hellenic civilization" considered their equal justification. Thinking men of the times understood at least the first of these tendencies in Roman nature, and it was from this fact that they so strenuously opposed the Greek games and the habits of their gymnasia. They felt sure of evil results, and the event proved that they were correct.

The answer to the question why these institutions of the Greeks were adopted leads to a connection of the facts we have just stated with the theory which our thesis supports. Evidently, there *Connection of this with Thesis* must have been an ideal which called for the adoption of Greek customs; and, in reality, these customs simply furnished new methods for the realization of the ideal of personal aggrandizement and enjoyment. No doubt, contact with the Greeks did a great deal to change Roman ideals. Yet

Greek civilization was essentially a new mode for Roman self-realization. And this is supported by the observation, common among historians, that the Romans of the later republic were trying to be Greeks, when they were not able.

At such a time, Augustus came into power. As soon as he had quietly gathered into his own hands all the reins of government, he found himself, as a result of the Greek influence, and the extent of his dominion, the master, not of the city of Rome, but of a Graeco-Roman empire. To be sure, the name was Rome; but the army was of diverse extraction, the intellectual life was predominantly Greek, and the morality was Greek, but unrefined, and with Oriental admixtures.

Character of the Augustan Empire

This was the first period of the empire, and we mark two others which were organic, the Age of the Antonines (96–186 B. C.), and the empire as perfected by Diocletian and Constantine. Between the first and second, there was the period of turmoil in the palace which resulted in the violent death of the majority of the reigning emperors, and between the second and third, the government was a military despotism.

Periods of the Empire

I—DEVELOPMENT OF THE IDEAL

The ideal in the time of Augustus, we have already substantially described. It was of personal enjoyment and called for more or less of culture. *Laissez faire* was its policy toward the state, but it instructed men to pursue the arts of the courtier; and those who were near the person of the emperor chiefly sought to stand first in his favor. There was the same attempt at display which we have noted, and the character of popular amusements was very low. The citizen claimed to be a citizen, not of Rome, but of the world — and someone has remarked that this attitude is usually "a cloak for selfishness." Only among the Stoics had the ideal what we to-day call a "moral" tone. The main thing was pleasure and advantage. The Stoics, indeed, present a somewhat remarkable spectacle, preaching (with or without practicing them) the principles of an elevated morality, in the midst of general vice and degradation. Yet, even their teaching, as their lives, was in the nature of a

Ideal in the Time of Augustus

compromise. Not the conquest of adverse circumstances, but the loosing of the bands of life with one's own hand, was the great remedy which they prescribed for human ills. And their decisions in the matter of particular duties were continually fluctuating.

In the time of the Antonines, the ideal was in many respects the same, but more content with a life of tranquility. The ideal demanded a certain amount of pleasure and excitement, but the tendency seems rather away from excess. Christianity, Stoicism, and Platonic philosophy were making steady headway, and they inculcated among all whom they influenced a new ideal of personality. So the ideal included a certain brotherhood of mankind; yet this was as much on the basis of common wrongs as on that of equal rights. Christians were here numerous enough to give a tinge to the ideal of the period. But still they were of their day as much as we all must be. Their living was an idealized selfishness, rather than an altruistic life. Thousands coveted for themselves the martyr's crown, and begged to receive it as the reward of faithful confession.[1] But in this there is no reproach; it was infinitely better than the conduct of multitudes around them.

<small>In the Time of the Antonines</small>

We may trace the ideal with a growth which is most apparent in matters of religion, on to the next organic period, the period of Constantine's empire. Now there was, apparently, a bursting forth of that side of the ideal which we marked in the later republic. Then there was a growing and intense desire for a positive religious belief. Greek philosophy and Oriental worships ministered somewhat to this longing. But in these later days, the spread of Christianity gave the ideal a common form, and furnished a means for its satisfaction. The life of the East, for the center of the empire was there, was strongly marked by religiosity. Even what interest there was in politics expressed itself in religious factions. But the ideal closely allied religion and dogma, and was of man as believing certain statements of truth, quite as much as doing certain things. The emphasis was on forms and not on character. Yet the ideal

<small>In the later Empire</small>

---

[1] So Kedney: Hegel's Æsthetics, p. 178. "There is many a so-called Christian martyr who has been so from Oriental or Pagan, rather than on purely Christian grounds."

demanded a greater purity of life and a broader sympathy, a truer feeling of humanity, than its predecessors.

To a somewhat remarkable degree, this period was a formative one in Eastern thought. The religious ideal found manifestation in ecclesiastical institutions peculiar to itself. The predominant emphasis on dogma and hierarchical rule, on forms and formularies, rather than the realities which they were designed to express, is apparent in the Greek, Nestorian, and Armenian churches, and to a less extent, in the church of Rome. And as we see the first three to-day, they stand in substance for this same ideal of the empire, which in religious matters still obtains in the East.

Its Persistence

Briefly, now, we may undertake to show the parallel development of institutions in the Roman Empire. It is, as we have elsewhere noted, characteristic of a monarchy that it can retain for a long time a single form of institution, while the ideal of the people is gradually changing. This we find true in the empire, and so the rate of apparent progress is very slow. Another cause of the slow progress is the wide extent of the Roman dominion. And a third fact which we should remember is that the ideal of the Augustan Age was the basis of the ideal in the two succeeding periods. There were, indeed, certain tendencies, as we have already shown, in these latter periods; but though some of them went deeper down, most of them were rather on the surface of society. The essence of the ideal was, all through, about the same. These things, accordingly, discourage our anticipation of very great or very positive progress; and expecting little, we shall not be disappointed, if more appears than that for which we look.

Preliminary as to Institutions

II—PARALLEL DEVELOPMENT OF INSTITUTIONS RELATING TO SUBJUGATION OF NATURE

First, as to material surroundings. We have already spoken of the luxury of the social aristocracy in the later days of the republic and in the empire under Augustus. Their dwellings rivaled the buildings of the state; they were adorned with all the ornaments which Greek ingenuity could devise, and Roman wealth and arms secure. It is characteristic of the suc-

Material Welfare— Empire under Augustus

ceeding reigns that the many estates which were confiscated were used to gratify the whims of the emperor; they were for his personal use. So there was an immense waste of money. The palace of Nero, built of gold, is a single example, and it may serve to illustrate the extravagant scale of every undertaking. But after society had secured itself during the first century, the reigns which we group under those of the Antonines show a much more tranquil condition. *Under Antonines* Wealth was apparently better distributed, and there were many who were able to spend their lives in the pursuit of literature and philosophy. Men seem to have been really Hellenized, so that it was possible for them with success to play the part of the Greek gentleman. In the military despotism which succeeded, such quiet elegance was impossible. The wealth of the empire was consumed by the lust of its princes, and the irresponsible authority and control of the army made almost any life precarious and continually in doubt.

When the empire was reorganized, all were equally ground down by the government. The main object of labor was to supply the taxes, which now had at least the formal justification of meeting the expenses of the court officials and of royalty. *Under Diocletian and Constantine* The officers and the emperor were the only persons of wealth. Ordinary citizens, if we may so designate them, could only make enough to keep up with the demands of the state, and this must be done whether the family had their needs supplied or not. In the capital, Constantinople, many public buildings arose, built from the imperial treasury. There were great displays and most magnificent entertainments, at the public expense, and the populace became wild in their excitement and enthusiasm. But for the body of the people, the provincials of outlying countries, there was only calamity and untold misery.

	CAUSALITY.	MATERIAL WELFARE
1	Luxury, palaces of rich and emperor, immense waste,	Due to ideal of display.
2	Better distribution of wealth,	To tendency away from excess, and certain brotherhood in ideal; but much to circumstances.
3	Officers and emperor alone wealthy; great displays at Constantinople, misery in provinces,	To continuing ideal of personal enjoyment; (perhaps to ideal of formal religiousness).

120   *IDEALS AND INSTITUTIONS*

Common Occupations— Under Augustus
So largely is the history which we possess confined to the government, and to the capitals of the empire, that it is difficult to learn much of the ordinary occupations. Rome, practically from first to last, sought amusement. Yet undoubtedly many devoted themselves to trade. The provincials were, as a class, thrifty in the days of Augustus. They contributed much to the greatness of the empire by their economic productiveness; in fact, they were the support of the city of Rome.

Under the Antonines
In the reigns of the Antonines, much the same was true; but owing to the thinning of the old races, more provincials than formerly had employment in the army. Numbers of the citizens followed polite literature, though only a few showed any considerable ability.

Under Constantine
Under Constantine, all were kept busy in labor for government support. And although Justinian, at a later day, encouraged commerce and many special industries, the people were being forced, by imperial taxation, into the lethargy of the Middle Ages. The city populaces of Constantinople, of Alexandria, and of Antioch took up and carried out the customs of Rome. The only new element was the influence of Christianity. And this had weight as the number of Christian artisans increased, and as the growth of the church made the occupation of the Christian minister a larger factor in social life.

	CAUSALITY.	COMMON OCCUPATIONS
1	Seeking amusement,	Due to ideal of personal enjoyment.
	Traders,	To ideal of personal gain remaining.
	Thrifty provincials,	To special ideals for each.
2	More provincials in army,	To *laissez faire* ideal.
	Philosophy and literature,	To new ideal of personality; also to opportunity and ideal of personal pleasure.
3	Labor to pay taxes,	To ideals of special provinces.
	Amusement-seeking city,	To personal enjoyment, still continuing.
	Christian ministry,	To ideal of religious life.
	Christian artisans as a distinct body	to the same.

III — PARALLEL DEVELOPMENT OF INSTITUTIONS RELATING TO SOCIAL ORGANIZATION

The institution of the family exhibits a wholesome development. It will be remembered that in the days of Augustus and his immediate successors, an immoral people found no fault with the vices of its rulers; rather, it took them as its examples. The efforts which the first emperor made to restore family life, and their ill-success, may also recur to mind. *The Family — Under Augustus*

But in the times of the Antonines, the changing ideal seems to have induced a new development of family life. Indeed, the vices of some of the emperors, more especially after this period, excited positive disgust among the people. Yet we are not to think that society was immediately renovated, or that it was restored to its original purity. Only in comparison with the life of the preceding century, it was somewhat cleansed. *Under the Antonines*

Undoubtedly a great part of this elevation of morality was due to the influence of Christianity. For instance, as making woman the possessor of an immortal soul, it placed her on an equal footing with man. And this same regard for woman marks the Greek romances, a literary feature of these times, which are said to be almost chivalrous in their tone. Christianity also forbade infanticide — for so long an insurmountable barrier to a pure and ennobling family life — and, in addition, obtained its royal discouragement. *Influence of Christianity*

In the life of the later empire, an indication of the activity of the new ideal, and yet of its intertwining with the old, is seen in the celibacy of the clergy, and the cognate teaching of the blessedness of perpetual virginity. Long before the time at which these were enjoined as Christian duties, such lives had been counted as of distinguished virtue, and undoubtedly they had been undertaken in protest against the dissoluteness of the world. But by their extreme position, they partook of the evils of their antagonists. Neither was the path of perfect virtue. And, in fact, asceticism, by removing the penitent from among men, destroyed the normal working of the leaven of Christian living. It must not be taken as an imputation against *Later Empire — Celibacy a Product of the times* the sincerity of these early saints, but their celibacy was also marked by the same ostentation as the vices of their depraved neighbors. The common ideal still held to the idea of realities as being the things which are apparent, almost external. The hermit in his lonely cave and Stylites on his pillar obtained reputation for their peculiar and ostentatious expressions of piety and religious fervor. The times required some great outward mark of a changed life and of separation from that which is evil. Both good and bad, pagan and Christian, wholly separated things social and physical from things spiritual. They had no adequate conception of the natural as the manifestation of the workings of the supernatural.

	CAUSALITY.	THE FAMILY
1	Immorality,	Due to ideal of personal, sensual gratification.
2	New development of family life, Woman on equality with man, Infanticide frowned on, Disgust at emperor's vices,	To ideal of personality, new, Christian. To same.
3	Celibacy of the clergy, Ostentatious piety,	To ideal of religious life. To ideal of display.

The State — Under Augustus

During the first two periods, the state was, in form, a constitutional empire, and in the third, an Oriental despotism. In the first epoch, Rome was the seat of government; and the glory of the city gave an added luster to the empire. But the imperial policy soon did away with the popular assemblies and made the senate the center of democratic power, and then that body was gradually weakened. The emperor centralized all civil power in his own hands. This transformation from the period of civil war to a well-ordered and secure government was, of course, hailed with delight; and — ill-omen — the people more and more relished military rule and called it strong government. It was under the succeeding Claudians, however, that the evil appeared. Augustus was himself a man of broad mind and intelligent statesmanship, but his successors forgot the true welfare of the people in catering to the public enjoyment or in ministering to their own desires. Bribery of senators became rife. The known attitude of the emperor intimidated men who were aware of the prudent and upright path, and who otherwise would have advocated it. Then the crimes of each emperor engendered within him a feeling of insecurity, and so *delatores* skulked everywhere in search of information as to the sovereign's enemies. Under the circumstances, we might expect that these rulers had little acquaintance with peace and tranquility. In fact, violence did reign supreme in the palace. Six of the first nine emperors fell by the assassin's hand. Of the three who ended their days according to nature, Augustus is his own memorial, Vespasian is characterized as having been a man of hardy virtue, and Titus as "one of the most accomplished and benevolent of men." But of the six, we find that Tiberius was, in the judgment of charity, a raging madman; Caligula surpassed the vices of Tiberius; Claudius, the tool of Messalina, was "a monster of wickedness"; Nero bore the stain of every crime of which human nature is capable; gluttony and coarse vices rendered Vitellius remarkable; and of Domitian it is enough to say that he possessed all the vices and cruelty of the Claudian family. Surely this was not a pleasing spectacle, from our modern point of view. But it did not greatly trouble the people, for "bread and shows" still continued.

At length, deliverance from these wicked rulers ushered in the Age of the Antonines. Rome was still the seat of the government, and, in a new sense, its center. Formerly the term "Roman" had excluded a great many. Now it excluded some, but a far smaller number. The senate was a body of dignity, and its official rites were more or less recognized. Its rolls bore the names of a goodly number of provincials, and its membership was fairly representative of the whole empire. Much of the political character of the old republic marked the government; in fact, it was under that name that men preferred to speak of it. Theoretically, the emperor was a president chosen for life. He was elected by the senate, with the consent of the soldiers, and was privileged to nominate, but could not appoint, his successor. There was, in general, harmony between the political and military organizations, both being able to center their affection and devotion upon a single man. Among the citizens at large there was nominally slavery to the emperor; but practically, there was comparative political freedom, and a great deal of pride was felt in the Roman rule.

Military Despotism

The military despotism which followed is indicative of the small place which politics really occupied in the ideal, and of the narrow idea which was commonly entertained, at any rate by the soldiers, of the duties of a sovereign. It was a hopeful sign that the people felt, even a little, the servitude to which they were being subjected, and that some of the emperors, and the Praetorians, awakened feelings of shame and resentment by their high-handed despotism. In these years of transition the empire was more and more overshadowing Rome. An edict of Caracalla extended the franchise to all within the Roman boundaries, and already the population of Rome was only a small percentage of that of the empire. Many of the emperors were not Romans by birth. Some of the most worthy were persons who a century and a half before would have been counted barbarians and fit only to be slaves. The vitality of the nation was in the provinces, and its hope was the advancing Northern tribes.

Diocletian and Constantine

In the Oriental empire, inaugurated by Diocletian and perfected by Constantine, we see the complete centralization of civil and military power. The preceding military despotism had reduced all other power before that of the soldiery. Now civil power was reorganized on a military basis. The result was an admirable governmental machine. The emperor became a sultan. Living in seclusion, he increased the dread and awe in which he was held by the difficulty of access to his person. He appointed his successor, and no one could gainsay. Amongst the people this imperial machine was an uniform crushing tyranny, and it stopped only with the limits of the empire. Now there was real political slavery, and a new official class was formed by the overseers and task-masters deputed by the throne.

End of the Old Roman Sway

The establishment of the government at Constantinople and the division of the empire mark the beginning of the end of Rome. Her most ambitious and noteworthy spectacles had been the triumphs of victorious generals, but the last of these was celebrated by Diocletian in 303. In the West the continued growth of the Gothic power ultimately prevailed, and accomplished the extinction of the Roman rule in 476. In the East the empire still persevered. The circus at Constantinople became the theater of struggles similar to those which Rome had witnessed. The factions of the circus had been imported from Italy, and were made a part of the city organization. The Whites were allied with the Blues, and the Reds with the Greens, and the two parties with the two divisions of the church. Each of the two factions had a regular organization, and any citizen might obtain membership. By these parties the people expressed their will in the circus, and so much is even a despotic prince subject to the will of the people, that Justinian is said to have been dependent for his position on the support of the Blues.

This great emperor marks the limit of the old Roman spirit. In a sense, his codification of the laws was the burial of the political vitality of the Roman empire, a sign that its law-making was over. And by his abolition of the XII Tables, he also marked the extreme of the old Roman sway. In 542, the great plague spread a sort of pall over the whole empire. Justinian applied himself more strictly to ecclesiastical affairs, and the army decayed for want of anything to do. The epoch was everywhere pervaded by a sort of foreboding gloom, as when, with the ominous mutterings and rumblings of distant thunder, the sky becomes overcast with heavy clouds.

It would be a serious omission to make no mention of the political influence of Christianity. The Christian, to be sure, had of himself no place in the ruling class. By the teachings of the Fathers, he was to suffer and to bear in patience the burdens of government. Nevertheless, by Christian emperors, the teachings of the new religion were gradually introduced into the workings of the state, and their trace is seen in the adoption of Christianity by Constantine, and in the Institutes of Justinian. Yet, a more important influence was the growth within the despotic imperialism of a republic of God, a state in which mutual love and friendship and a common charity were enthroned to reign supreme, as the laws of God revealed to men. This was a new political life, and therefore a vital force, in the midst of the old and dying state. And alone of all the organizations of Rome, this was able to survive the shock of barbarian invasion, and the darkness of the mediæval age.

Political Influence of Christianity

	CAUSALITY.	THE STATE
1	Centralization of civil power, strong government,	Due to ideal of personal enjoyment *laissez faire*.
	Bribery of senators,	To ideal of personal gain.
	Intimidation,	Of imperial favor and self-interest.
	This, *delatores*, violence in palace,	To ideal of personal aggrandizement.
2	" Roman " constituency broader,	To ideal of personality and brotherhood.
	Senate dignified and representative,	To same.
	Real freedom, though nominal political slavery,	To ideal of personality.
	Military despotism,	To ideal of personal power and *laissez faire*.
	All in empire Romans,	To ideal of personality and brotherhood. (On emperor's part, to ideal of personal gain.)
	Barbarian emperors,	To ideal of personality.
3	Oriental despotism,	To ideal of personal aggrandizement, enjoyment, and display.
	Religious factions,	To ideal of religiousness in form, and to new ideal of personality.
	Republic of God,	To Christian ideal — new ideal of personality in its pure and best form.

Religion Under Augustus

But Christianity was first a new religion, and its primary effect is witnessed in religious institutions. We have seen how prevalent were skepticism and foreign superstition in the time of Augustus. Political habit made men stand by the rites of the Roman religion, but at heart they despised it all. Stoic philosophy taught that a man should duly perform the religious ceremonies of his own country. But the Stoic himself made philosophy his real religion, and in his view the educated classes generally shared. So far as they found any consolation or hope, it was in the uncertain teachings of these theorists. Yet, hand in hand with this agnosticism and discrediting of the national divinities, we find most abject belief in omens and portents. There seems to have been a sort of medley of Oriental superstitions swaying men's minds. How just were the conceptions of religion, of its place and its value, may be judged from the apotheosis of the emperors. Simply a matter of political policy, it degraded religion even below a blind devotion to humanity. And this really grew worse in the succeeding reigns, when not good rulers only, but men most infamous, received, with scarcely an exception, the customary deification.

In the Age of the Antonines, however, Christianity exercised a positive influence as a religion. Many still worshiped in the old ways, a large number frequented the shrines of Oriental divinities, many sought consolation in the teachings of the philosophers. *Age of the Antonines* But none of these, to any extent, made proselytes. Christianity alone asserted its inherent power by the enrolling of recruits under its standards. A critical test of any religion is its ability to stay human fears in the last hours of mortal life, the view, namely, which it takes of death. Roman religion, naturally, had little to offer here; it was only a ritual on a political basis. Oriental beliefs magnified life and centered attention in it. The Stoics glorified the fact of death as the doorway out of life, a release from the world's burdens. But Christianity taught that men were to use life, and then to welcome death as the entrance into a still continuing life beyond the grave. For this world is taught contentment, cheerfulness, and deeds of charity, and to those who were weary and sick at heart, it offered an abiding consolation. Hence, in one particular, its superiority. It is worth noting, too, that, for the first time in the history of Greece or Rome, religion was brought forward as the inspiration and sanction of a reform. This shows the higher ethical ground of Christianity, as well as its hold upon the nation.

From these facts we expectantly look forward to a great development in religion, but we do not find it along the lines in which we might anticipate. The ideas of Christianity failed to obtain free play. *Time of Constantine* They were mingled with those of the generation. And so what was full of promise for social morality was contracted and restrained. There was a vigorous spirit of religion and morality, religion excited much more interest than politics; but theology was the predominant power. The heat of religious fervor was spent in polemical debates, and the subject of these disputes was not paganism or sin, as this might appear in conduct, but heretical dogma. The fact which is most commonly caught up as peculiarly marking this Age of Constantine is the adoption of Christianity as the state religion. Certainly this meant much, and we should not underrate its real importance. Whatever the emperor's motive may have been, it is indicative of a new ideal that this religion did not seek political support, but that, perchance, the emperor desired the undergirding of the new faith for the authority of the empire.

	CAUSALITY.	RELIGION
1	Formal religion a political habit,	Due to remnant of ideal of early Rome, and citizenship.
	Various religions,	Due to particularistic standpoint of ideal.
	Abject belief in portents,	To ideal of ease and enjoyment.
	Deification of emperors,	To ideal of imperial favor, form of that of personal gratification.
2	Many worship in old ways,	Due to old ideas, strengthened by reflex of new ideal of personality.
	Synchretizing process,	To ideal as recognizing a certain brotherhood; and of personality.
	Christianity sets up a higher ethical standard; is a positive converting force; religion basis of political reform.	To new ideal of personality, the Christian ideal.
3	No vigorous development of Christianity, theology predominating	To ideal of form rather than life.
	Adoption of Christianity as state religion,	To ideal of religiousness on people's part; also of personal gain on part of emperor.

Society — Caste Distinctions

Next in order are the customs of society, the institutions of slavery and caste distinctions. Of the last, it may be said at the outset that the empire was unfavorable to them. There was but one established division, the emperor and the people. But there were other contributing causes. One was that the rich young men quickly wasted their wealth, and that proscriptions early removed all men of dangerous estate or position. Another, was the general circulation of people from all the universe through Rome. "She received them slaves, and sent them back Romans." So it was that the distinctions of the republic were rapidly broken down, and in practical life high birth counted for very little. Some of the richest — and therefore noblest — men after Caligula were freedmen, and one of the most ornate tombs which has been discovered on the Appian way was erected by a freedwoman of the early empire. Yet there is here, as one might infer, the division into rich and poor, the basis for a distinction in position and privileges, though not in rights. In the time of the Antonines, the body of the Italian residents formed, in a sense, a middle class, a sort of aristocracy of culture. And there was still in men's minds a broad distinction between Romans and barbarians. But under

Constantine, this separation had disappeared. "Roman" had become only a name; it lacked the old significance. The people of the empire in this later period constituted a body of imperial servants, and aside from them, there was only an official class, composed largely of Orientals, who executed to the letter the commands of their master.

	CAUSALITY.	CASTE
1	Strong caste divisions,	Due to ideal of personal enjoyment and display.
2	Little caste intensity, middle class of Italian residents,	To new ideal of personality, and to tendency away from excess.
	Line between Romans and barbarians letting down,	To ideal of brotherhood.
3	All members of empire Romans,	To same increasing; broader sympathy.
	All imperial servants,	Of personal gain on part of emperor; of ease on people's part (?).

Slavery was, under Augustus, a most cruel and degrading institution. Slaves were many. They had, practically, no rights. They were considered simply as "vocal instruments." And yet, the possibility of manumission, the common result of faithful service, mitigated somewhat the hardships of their lot. The tranquil Age of the Antonines witnessed enactments in favor of slaves. Perhaps the most important was the establishment by Hadrian that slaves had some rights before the law. More attention was paid to their training, and in consequence, their condition was much ameliorated, and not a few of them occupied positions of responsibility. Many of the best educators of Rome were slaves. Undoubtedly, the decrease in the number of captives, and the consequent dependence on the natural increase of the slave population, had something to do with the milder and more humane treatment. Stoicism, too, had some influence. But the great power was Christianity, as it inculcated new ideas of humanity, of what it meant and whom it included, and so modified the old ideal. In Constantine's empire, the whole body of the people were reduced to the condition of agricultural serfs. But the distinction between slave and free still remained — now only a matter of the degree of servitude. We note, in Justinian's reign, that the number of ways in which a slave might be manumitted was increased. And this may serve us as a sign, embedded in the legislation of the times, of the leaven of Christian humanity.

CAUSALITY.	SLAVERY
1 Cruel treatment; slaves many, degraded,	Due to ideal of enjoyment, display, and personal ease.
2 Rights of slaves at law, better training, responsible positions.	New ideal of personality, Christian.
3 All subjects agricultural serfs, though distinctions in servitude remain	Due to ideal of personal gain.
Increase of ways of manumission,	To Christian ideal, broader sympathy.

Social Customs

The social customs of the empire present but few great variations. In general the development was toward purity and away from cruelty.

The gladiatorial games marred the first two periods, and we shudder at their barbarity, unparalleled among educated peoples. But under Constantine, they were put down, and instead great spectacles were provided. In the Age of Antonines, a change apparently had already begun. It may be that by continual reading we grow accustomed to the monotonous recital of imperial benefactions, and we do not give its true weight to the oft-repeated tale of bread and shows, shows and bread. But it really seems as though life at this time had somewhat regained its balance, and as though there was a general abstention from excess. In these happy reigns there was, too, considerable freedom in family and social life, apparently a fresh and vigorous development. But the new brood of emperors rendered it short-lived. It was not until the Christian empire that it could grow at all. In the time of Augustus, the lives of her citizens still bore the marks of Rome. But under Constantine, the forces of the East and the far West had their effect. The most apparent of the new characteristics were Oriental softness and effeminacy, which the former engendered in the Asiatic provinces, and Gothic rudeness and turmoil, which ruled in the West and reveled in the rich bed of the decaying civilization. Yet, to the latest days, there was a common temper among the people. All along, a large proportion of the Romans were maintained and amused at the public expense, and at any time it would have been safer for the emperor to omit the distributions of corn, than the spectacles for the entertainment of the people.

	CAUSALITY.	CUSTOMS
1	Gladiatorial games, Roman life of entertainment.	Due to ideal of personal pleasure.
2	Gladiatorial games, but more balance,	To new ideal of personality, growing and appearing as tendency away from excess.
	Family and social life developed,	To new ideal of personality.
3	Great spectacles instead of gladiatorial games	To Christian ideal.
	Oriental life in court,	To ideal of pleasure and ease (from Eastern peoples).
	Gothic life,	Likewise to native ideals; see early Teutonic.

Possibly the most compact summary in which to bring this development before our minds is by the grouping together of its characteristic places and personalities. The latter may present the ideals of the different ages, and the former their institutions; and their correspondence will be at once allowed.

Typical places are: of the first period, Rome and Baiæ; of the second, Rome, Alexandria, and Corinth; and of the third, Alexandria, Antioch, and Constantinople.

Typical characters are: of the Augustan Age, Augustus, Seneca, and Livia; of that of the Antonines, Pliny the Younger; and of the later epoch, Constantine — who may stand, by opposition, for the provincials — and John Chrysostom, sometime bishop of the Eastern capital.

For Summary, see also the following chart:

PERIOD	IDEAL	INSTITUTIONS RELATING TO							TYPICAL	
		SUBJUGATION OF NATURE			SOCIAL ORGANIZATION				INDIVIDUAL CULTURE	
		Material Welfare	Common Occupations	Family	State	Religion	Social Customs	Education	Persons	Places
Early Empire	**Display.** Personal enjoyment. *Laissez faire.* Imperial favor.	Luxury. Extravagance.	Amusement in city; also trade. Thrifty provincials.	Looseness. Immorality.	Centralization of power.—"Strong" government. Bribery and intimidation. Use of gov't for popular pleasure. Violence in palace. *Delatores.*	Formal religion a political habit. Stoic philosophy. Abject belief in portents. Deification of emperors.	*Caste*—Conditions unfavorable to rank, but not to classes on basis of wealth. *Slavery*—Many slaves; cruelty, but possibility of manumission. *Custom*—Marks of Rome on life of empire. Gladiatorial games.	Much the same as in the later Republic.	Augustus, Seneca. Livia.	Rome. Baiæ.
Age of the Antonines	**Same, with tendency away from excess.** Higher sense of personality. A certain brotherhood of mankind. With many, Christian.	Wealth better distributed.	Same. More provincials in army.	New development of family life. Disgust at vices of emperors.	"Roman" excludes some. Senate representative. Much of old republican character. Nominally political slavery, but really freedom. High-handed military despotism. Extension of franchise. Barbarian emperors.	Many worship in old ways. Syncretizing process. Christianity a positive influence; it spreads; a conversing power. Religion for the first time made the basis of a moral reform.	*Caste*—In a sense, all form a middle class. *Slavery*—Enactments in favor of slaves. Better training, more humane treatment. *Custom*—Gladiators; but less excessive excitement. Fresh development of social life; soon killed out.	But with the addition of	Pliny the Younger.	Rome. Alexandria. Corinth.
Later Empire	**Same, with strong religious tendency, but toward form more than character.** Greater purity and broader sympathy.	Emperor and officials only persons of wealth. Display and extravagance in city; misery in provinces.	Provincials labor for gov't support. Populace of cities copy customs of Rome. Increased number of Christian artisans and ministers.	Christianity elevated woman. In general, more purity. Christian celibacy; extreme.	Oriental empire. Uniform, crushing tyranny. Religious factions. Growth within the despotism of a republic of God—the church.	Not the vigorous growth of Christianity which we expect. Theology predominates; adoption of Christianity as state religion. For first time Roman state seeks support of religion.	*Caste*—Whole body of empire=imperial servants; also official class. *Slavery*—Whole people slaves; only degrees in servitude. Justinian increases modes of manumission. *Custom*—Spectacles. Some growth of social life. Oriental softness in East; Gothic rudeness in West.	Christian elements.	Constantine. John Chrysostom.	Alexandria. Antioch. Constantinople.

CHAPTER IV

THE PARALLEL DEVELOPMENT OF TEUTONIC IDEALS AND INSTITUTIONS

The problem which history since the fall of the Western Roman Empire presents to us is by no means simple. It touches occurrences fourteen centuries apart. It has to do with a multitudinous and widely-scattered population. Its development is seen, not in the progress of a single nation, but in the growth of numerous barbarian tribes. Were we to attempt to trace each tribe with the change in its ideal and institutions (if that were not well-nigh impossible), the undertaking would be too vast. But, fortunately, there is one race-family, the Teutonic, which has shaped the destiny of Europe ; and for our purposes, we may consider the development of European civilization as, in general, that of the Teutonic race. If objection be made to this position, justification may be found in the facts of a common barbarism, and of a common contact more or less slight with Rome, before the sixth century, and in the consideration that "Teutonic" is here used in a representative rather than an exact sense. It stands, in general, for that whole body of barbarians from whom have sprung the Western Europeans of to-day. *Preliminary— Difficulties*

In Roman civilization, in order to note the true development, we began, not when Greece first came in contact with or strongly influenced the city, but with the early fathers of the state. So in European history, we commence with the early life of the Teutonic tribes, and learning thus their primitive ideals and institutions, we obtain the basis for the developments of mediæval and modern history. The most natural division into periods seems to be : *Divisions of Teutonic History*

    I. Primitive Teutonic, to 400 A. D.
    II. Romano-Teutonic or Transitional, 400–500.
    III. Dark Ages, 500–1100.
    IV. Restoration of Order, 1100–1400.
    V. Revolution and Re-adjustment, 1400—.

To-day, in a very true sense, we are still in the Middle — though not the Dark — Ages, for the elements of modern social order have not yet crystalized. Feudalism was an organic stage of society, but not so our organization to-day. Between that time and this, there has been going on the preparation for a new society. And the manifestations of a Teutonic ideal in a Teutonic race, as in the German Empire and the American Republic, are the signs of a new political life and an era of widespread personal self-realization.

As has been our custom, we shall first present the development of the moral ideal, and then show the parallel development of institutions.

I — THE DEVELOPMENT OF THE IDEAL

In the early Teutonic days, the chief element of the ideal of the half-savage barbarian was personal prowess. Attention was concentrated on activity; certain things were to be done, and he simply did them. A double sphere of life, however, gave to this ideal two diverse colorings. The first was domestic. The ideal man was a member of a family, and as such he was strong in defending and advancing its interests. It was from the nature of the family that the idea of duty took its origin, and about the family hearth the first lessons concerning duty were learned. Even the child was made to feel the call of the family for fidelity, truthfulness, and loyalty to duties. And later, he saw that courage was exalted, while the coward was despised, and experienced the demand for economy, for uprightness, and for purity in the life of the home. How weighty was the sanction which these obligations thus received, we may judge from the fact that a punishment heavier than death was expulsion from the family, and that parricide was considered peculiarly horrible and infamous.

Primitive Teutonic Ideal

The second sphere of life was public. The ideal man was a member of a military organization. Here he was, of course, preferably a leader, yet he knew how to be a loyal follower. In either case, an intense love of personal independence and individual freedom marked his conduct. The ideal chief had wealth and immense tribute, great power, and a mighty fame; but more important, was that without which these possessions never came, a warlike spirit and undaunted courage. And the leader stood for what each of his followers desired. One and all, these Teutons have well been characterized as "Gentes periculorum avidas." The instinct to fight seems to have been inborn. Fighting was "the sport of children, the rivalry of youth, the habit of age." To play, to dance, to fight — all these, our English word "lark" expressed to them. And what they conceived as the height of happiness was not essentially different, the "dream," the blitheness when the horn began to go round and song and merry wassail occupied. In many respects it was the counterpart of the clash of arms and the intense excitement of the battlefield.

Of course we do not expect perfection, or anything like it, from these "children of the forest." As Kingsley says, "They were only big boys, having the passions and lacking the restraints of men." Yet it is evident that they did possess a certain real nobility and steadfastness and independence, a courage, a loyalty, and a purity which make us honor them in spite of their pride and their boasting, their ignorance and their love of bloodshed. Their ideal was largely external, and the goods which they valued were chiefly of the body, yet there was a touch of higher feeling. The note is worth the making, too, that while the Teutons were guilty of many evil deeds, their vices sprang not from moral exhaustion, but from coarseness, and that coarseness can be refined. Their abundant life and activity were surely the promise of much greater things.

The fifth century A. D. was, roughly speaking, the period of the barbarian invasions, the time at which the Teutons first came into close and direct contact with Rome. The result was a rather decided change in the ideal. Emphasis was thrown on pleasure as the end of life, and the tendency to feasting and drinking, which had formerly terrified even the Romans, took high rank among the desires that were to be gratified. In general, there was, as in the earlier age, a predominance of the idea, that a man's life consists in the things which he has. Yet, side by side with this, was a growing respect for old age, even though the aged person was weak and feeble. There was, too, an increasing sense of man as in some political relations, and the gradual acquirement of a feeling of proprietor-

Transitional Period

ship, which, in the next period, was ready on the one hand to assert, and on the other to allow, the absolute right of mediæval royalty.

From the fifth century to the twelfth, from the time when the barbarians had settled down to work out their mission to the beginning of the recovery from the almost fatal decline of the year 1000, the ideal was the satisfaction of individual selfish aims. In the leaders, there was ambition for personal power; in the people at large insatiable cupidity. The great tendency of the times was away from centralization. Charlemagne, like a meteor, served only to make visible the darkness of the political sky. Among men in general, there was no conception of government as administrative, and very little of it as legislative. They thought of it chiefly as an authority for punishing wrongdoing; and the limitation was added that punishment must not be allowed to interfere with a person's freedom. Nor was the ideal of high attainment. It was of bodily strength and safety, of plunder and pillage. Yet there was something good. Harm and steal if you can, was the teaching, but openly. Sneaking, treachery, and cowardice were greatly despised. Private ethics was tinged, albeit never so slightly, with Christianity. And after a little the rough men learned not to sack the monasteries, and even viewed them with a sort of holy awe. Yet, at the end of this period, we find that the ideal recognized force instead of law, and that the two principles of society were land and the sword. Every man who had the power did as he pleased. Action was willful and capricious, and without co-operation.

Dark Ages

Somewhere about the beginning of the twelfth century, we enter on the restoration of society, and the 300 years that follow mark the organic stage of mediæval civilization. The spirit of the times was that of privilege. The predominant characteristic of the ideal seems to have been high position in a social-military order. At first, this position was valued in itself for the power it brought and the ability it gave to gratify personal desires. But soon, its various possibilities were followed out in the directions in which they led, and it was made to serve as the ground for divers military undertakings, immediately, pri-

Restoration of Order. Feudal Society — Predominant Ideal

vate wars, then the crusades, and lastly the glorious fulminations of chivalry. Yet, of course, this was not the ideal unmixed. It was power combined with ambition, and the feeling of personal rights that at first obtained the position. The ideal in its particularization was a curious combination of the principles of Feudalism, Christianity, and Chivalry. Of the whole, Christianity was nominally the center, and the virtues of Feudalism and Chivalry were such as the church could approve. Feudalism enjoined truth-speaking, and the troubadours sang of God as "the God who never lies." The crusades were an opportunity offered by the church for the satisfaction of military ambition, and liberality and frankness were demanded of the knights of chivalry. Yet the church was only the representative of Christianity; and neither the church nor the crusades which it planned were governed wholly by the highest motives. For the popes were not free from the ambition to rule. The temporal power was, to their minds, the completion and security of papal authority. Among the people, no doubt religious motives stirred some to crusade. But the hope of lands moved others, the military spirit led not a few, still others went on account of political reasons, and many made the journey for plunder — all of which, to say nothing of motives even more despicable, were hardly very high incentives to the performance of a Christian duty.[1] It may from this be inferred that the ideal was still largely external. For instance, in the twelfth century the chief and common desire for the boys of the day was physical strength, and a little later, strength and elegance. And yet we must not underrate the frankness which was demanded, and the odium with which deceit was met when it was discovered. The ideal may not have demanded mildness, or other things which we perhaps consider more essential, but it did demand a *measure* of morality.

Meantime, two other ideals were being conserved for the time of their manifestation, one in the communes — the ideal of popular government and of a life of labor and trade, and the other in the church — the ideal of equality and of social unity. In the last part of this period, they began to unfold and

<small>Other Ideals latent in Communes and Church —</small>

---

[1] A letter from Alexis of Constantinople to the Count of Flanders urges as reasons for crusading, "amor auri et argenti et pulcheriniarum fœminarum voluptas."

to take a place in the prevailing ideal of Europe. The first to exert a strong influence, was the ideal of the Free Cities.¹ These last years had witnessed a decay of the chivalrous sentiments, a decided lessening in enthusiasm, and a lowering in the popular morals. For a time, men were seemingly unconscious of what they were doing. Finally, however, they awoke to a desire for genuine order and comfort. Many embraced the ideal of the cities, and it became a formative element in mercantile and political life. It was at this time, also, that artisans and merchants began to be considered as good as knights. The barriers of society were beginning to crumble — sign of a new period and a new ideal.

In the next, and last, era — that of modern history — the ruling mark of the ideal seems to be the conscious realization of individuality. Man is recognized at first, and in increasing measure, as man, in all the broad significance of that inclusive term. The struggle for freedom moves from realm to realm of human life, and in each case it is individualistic. The ideal places emphasis upon individual rights in relation to the existing order. Already, as we have just said, business and trade were opening. The ideal pictured man as conquering nature, and making a livelihood from his surroundings. The first forward movement was in intellectual affairs. Men must be intellectually free; this was the ideal of the Renaissance. Freedom from authority, both for the individual and for the nation, was the ideal of the Reformation; and continued in the form of liberty of conscience it was seen in the deeds of the Pilgrim Fathers and in the English Revolution. The emphasis of the ideal was next on freedom of social and political life, in the time of the American and French revolutions. And last is the predominance of freedom of social life, which is, in general, the aim to-day.

<small>Revolution and Readjustment — Modern History</small>

In another way of putting it, the Teutonic ideal of the last 500 years has been a person as a person,² and while the conception of personality has been continually widening, it has yet

---

¹ This statement may be questioned, and the fact cited that the church had a great influence all through the Middle Ages. But it will be universally allowed that the ideal of social unity and of the equality of all men has not exercised a very strong control, until comparatively recent years; and this is the especial ideal that was being *conserved* in the church.

² It is possible that to some minds this phrase, "the ideal of man as man," or of "a person as a person" will not convey a distinct idea. It signifies (1) that men are conscious of themselves as individual personalities, *i. e.*, as men; and (2) that therefore they consciously seek the realization of personality as personality, *i. e.*, individual self-realization.

always remained generically the same. The desire to *be* has been, on the whole, more characteristic than the desire for possessions. First, the emphasis was upon intellectual capacities, next it touched the religious nature, then political, and, lastly, social life. And the effect has been cumulative. Each new attribute has been, indeed, an addition to that which preceded, so that to-day the ideal includes more than ever before, and a man is more of a man. Meantime, there has been also a differentiation between public and private life, an advance from the time when everything was for the king. And while the common ideal has yet much of selfishness and the love of conquest is still strong, the objects of pursuit have certainly changed with the slow refinement of human nature. The teachings of Christianity are now more widely received and practiced, and the feeling of the brotherhood of all mankind is now more general than ever before has been the case in the development of humanity upon the earth.

II — PARALLEL DEVELOPMENT OF INSTITUTIONS RELATING TO SUBJUGATION OF NATURE

Now giving our attention to institutions, we first consider those habits of social life which have to do with material welfare ; and in them we find the manifestation of the developing characteristics of the ideal. The early Teuton had a house which was his own, and even before he possessed what we should call the foretaste of comfort, he began to adorn this, his home. Of course, there was little chance for luxury in any direction. Only in selecting skins for clothing he always exercised great care, and his ornaments, though few and rude, were some of them of gold. Yet, in his way, he had comfort, enough to eat, and clothing to wear. Material Welfare —400

In the short period of transition, the old customs were in a manner swept away. The barbarians gained a new idea of life in its material aspects. A comfort and luxury, a gorgeous display which they had not before conceived was all around them, and they reveled in its pleasures. They accepted without reflection the things which it gave them, and their principal habit became that of taking what they could get without labor. Naturally they 400-500 showed some little elevation, from contact with their new surroundings, but they did not rise above them.

So it came to pass that in the Dark Ages there was general rudeness and poverty. There was no systematic attempt to till the soil, and people lived, in the main, from hand to mouth. Charlemagne tried to bring order out of the great individualization, but he did not succeed. More permanently useful were the monks, who, far out in the wilds of the forests, cleared broad fields, built themselves monasteries, and spent their lives in showing the people how to coax from the earth the products of the fertile soil. The material condition of the times may be seen from the fact that of the seventy years from 970 to 1040, forty were years of either famine or plague. Moreover, there were in this period the inroads of the Northmen, and the ideal, with its emphasis upon personal gratification, made impossible the organization of any great force which might be opposed to them. With impunity they laid waste much country.

<small>500 1100</small>

It was toward the close of this period, and in the next, that the castle appeared. Previously the houses had been, we have reason to think, a great improvement on primitive times. But of the Feudal Age, the castle was typical. Usually it occupied the brow of some hill, and so commanded a broad range of vision. Its battlements were significant of feuds and private wars, and its great halls of the bands of armed retainers. At the foot of the hill were clustered the huts of the serfs, and as compared with the lofty walls of stone, they manifested the ideal of the times and exhibited the humble position of their occupants. Material wealth increased for the lords in the time of the crusades. In the twelfth century there was considerable luxury. The decoration of the houses was quite ornate, both within and without. Yet all was coarse, rather than elegant. In the fourteenth century, likewise, we see great luxury and extravagance among the nobility and clergy, and wretchedness among the peasants.

<small>1100 1400</small>

But the peasants were beginning to realize their rights as men, as the Jacquerie bore savage testimony. And soon things began to change for the better.

<small>1400 —</small>

By 1450, there was a broader diffusion of movable wealth; and on down to our own day, the advance which is commonly marked above all others is that in material welfare. No longer needed for defence, the battlements of the feudal castles were soon turned into turrets and ornaments. The explorations of the voyagers, the invention of gunpowder and the invention of printing created a material revolution. This was perfectly in harmony with the new ideal of man as man, first exhibited now in the field of intellect; and the value of these innovations would have been little, but for the presence of the same ideal. Yet it was not till the French Revolution that man was able to work out his desires, as regarded material nature, with any sort of freedom. In 1780 France was owned by her upper classes. One three-hundred-and-twenty-fifth of the population owned one-fifth of the land. The clergy and the nobility had in their power two-thirds of her domain; one-fourth of her arable land lay fallow. The agricultural system was still practically that of the tenth century, and increased taxation was the only inducement held out by prosperity. Then the ideal which had been gathering power for so long had its manifestation in the French Revolution. In a few days, the old gave place to the new, and there was the beginning of greater material welfare for the French people. To-day, we have not reached the limit. Modern discoveries have, for practical purposes, largely annihilated space; they have made impossibilities realities, and the commonplaces of other days well-nigh impossible. Yet there are unknown storehouses of wealth and power still before us, to be conquered and rendered useful, as we are able to enter upon their occupancy. The high ideal of man as man, and the methods prevalent in the subjugation of nature are still progressing, as they have thus far developed, side by side.

	CAUSALITY.	MATERIAL WELFARE
1	House of his own, . .	Corresponds to ideal of man as member of family.
	Some adornment and comfort,	In their nature to warrior ideal; but in themselves to circumstances.
2	Borrowed splendor, . . .	Due to ideal of pleasure.
3	Rudeness and poverty, . . .	Due to individual selfish aims.
4	Castle, wealth and ornateness but not elegance. Huts, and misery of peasants and serfs, . . .	To ideal of privilege, and previous continuing.
5	Greater diffusion of movable wealth,	To ideal of personality of all.
	Discovery and invention, . .	To ideal of personality in each man.
	Breaking up of old agricultural system, ...	To ideal of a person as a person.

This is further apparent in the common occupations which engaged men. The business of the primitive Teuton was war; hunting furnished additional employment, and to some extent a recreation.

<small>Common Occupations—400</small>

The care of the home and the farm was given over to the women. They also, with their slaves, were the tailors and cobblers, and to them any writing was assigned. The only reputable handicraft for a man was the forging of armor and weapons. Hence the smiths were the honorable artisans. Of commerce, there was a little, but it was fitful and fragmentary. It is easy to see how all this centers about the ideal of man as a warrior, and the support of the family and the tribe as the bounden duty of all. For this reason the barbarian traders would be few and far between, for such men would have to forsake their tribal relations.

The Romano-Teutonic period does not show a marked change in occupations. No doubt a good many learned more thoroughly the methods of agriculture.

<small>400–500</small>

Yet in the main, the advance for those who came into closest contact with Rome was in the elevation of pleasure-seeking and of the gratification of personal desires into an occupation.

So it came about that in the next period, the ideal of personal, willful satisfaction makes any sort of classification difficult and uncertain. The clergy declared at one time, by their actions, if not by their words, that idleness was holy, and at another they made sporadic attempts to instruct the barbarians. Charlemagne would have had agriculture an established custom, but the people did not so will. And after his death, it was the old story of feud and revenge as the main pursuits of everyone who had the power. Serfs and vassals were set at tilling the soil; but not because they desired to do so — rather because it was the command of their lord.

<small>500—1100</small>

The further manifestations of the feudal ideal (the last statement in the preceding paragraph falls also under this paragraph as well) in the crusades and in chivalry affected, of course, the common occupations. They stimulated the trade of the armorer and the business of making equipments. The crusades threw the care of the great estates into new hands, and so infused fresh

<small>1100—1400</small>

life and vigor into agriculture. They also gave to commerce a powerful impetus, furnishing new materials and new methods. There was, too, the beginning of a movement towards fixed limits of work for corresponding wages. But at the same time there were the restrictions of powerful corporations, for instance, the Hanseatic League and the company of the Seine; and in the Free Cities there grew up monopolies and guilds which were ultimately inimical to industry. Here, as in the feudal system, the chief thing was position in an order, and only those who belonged to the guilds could exercise the various crafts.

This continued far into the next period, till finally the new ideal touched occupations too. Then there was a wonderful development in the number of employments. The exaggerated regulations of labor and trade, one by one, have been removed. And particularly in these later days, there are opening new avenues of business, and in the old paths, fresh opportunities. But the end of this is not yet; the ideal is still at work.

1400.—

	CAUSALITY.	COMMON OCCUPATIONS
1	War, hunting, forging weapons only,	Corresponds to ideal of warrior, of personal prowess.
	Little commerce,	To ideal of man as member of family.
2	Pleasure seeking,	Due to ideal of personal pleasure. Grew perhaps out of individual freedom of early ideal.
	New impetus to agriculture,	To old ideal of man as member of family.
3	Objection to agriculture, clergy idle and fluctuating, feuds and revenge, serfs compelled by their lords to till the soil,	To ideal of individual, selfish aims and their satisfaction.
4	Trade and commerce, manufacture, rise of agriculture,	To ideal of life of labor and trade, chiefly conserved in communes.
	Corporations and guilds,	To ideal of privilege.
5	Division of labor,	To ideal of man as individual man.
	Removal of exaggerated regulations from labor and trade,	To man as truly man.
	Fresh opportunities,	To ideal of man, in light of newer and fuller views of personality.

III — PARALLEL DEVELOPMENT OF INSTITUTIONS RELATING TO SOCIAL ORGANIZATION

The Teutonic family organization, manifesting the warrior ideal, rested on the capacity, or the prospective capacity, for bearing arms. Women, therefore, were not members of the tribe. Yet they were looked on as man's equals, in courage and mor-

The Family—
Primitive Teutonic

ality, and as his superiors even in prudence. They were reverenced as almost sacred, and were assigned a peculiar power and dignity. "Indeed," says Tacitus, "the German thinks there dwells in his women something holy and prophetic; he neither spurns their advice nor neglects their oracular sayings." They seem to have mediated between the human and the divine. "Men are for deeds," was the saying, "and women are for wisdom." And first looked on as sybils, with growing superstition they came to be regarded even as goddesses. It is not strange, then, that there was an odor of sanctity about the household, that marriage was deemed a sacred thing, and that there was general purity of life. In the case of a chief, to be sure, more than one wife was allowed, as a peculiar honor; for the ruling motive in these matters was apparently not moral feeling or love, but honor, economy, and dignity. Sentiment had but little place in marriage. Yet above this there shines brightly its inviolability and the general purity. Divorces were rare, and the punishments meted out to unfaithful wives were public and severe. Marriage ties, indeed, were used to cement political alliances, and Augustus thought no hostages so trusty and valuable as noble Teutonic women. At a very early stage, wives were obtained by capture, but later, though in still barbarian times, a price was substituted. Intermarriage was not allowed between serfs and free persons. When a free woman married a serf, either she was degraded to his level, or he was killed and she made a slave, or both were put to death.

In the family, the father was in control. He was responsible for the harm done to its members, and for all wrongs committed by them. By his position he was also the family highpriest. In accord with the physical nature of the ideal, it was customary to expose new-born children, if they were sickly, though this might not be done after food had passed their lips. Likewise, old and feeble men and women were customarily put out to die.

In the brief period of direct Roman influence, the main change was in the yielding of the warriors to the excesses of savage conquest, and to the corrupting influences of Italy. There was a great degeneration in morality; and this became even more apparent in the next era.

Transitional Period

At least up to 800, divorce *sine causa sontica* was common. The influence of the church in this period was predominantly not for the good. Celibacy of the clergy was the rule, but it was considered more important that the priests should not marry formally than than that they should live lives of purity. And when they were corrupt, who could advise and reprove the people. Their spiritual and moral counsellors were become their examples in evil. Another fact which boded ill for the family was the enforcement by Carl the Great of his will, and of the royal tutelage against that of the household. Other authority, both individual and domestic, was made to yield before that of the king. We remember that the men of these times were willful and passionate, and we are not surprised that, when his strong hand was removed, they lapsed into moral degradation greater than before.

<small>Dark Ages</small>

But the Feudal system and the growth of the ideal of power through position gave a new impulse, though indirectly, to family life. The members of his family were the only companions of the lord through the long winter, so by force he became well acquainted with them, and learned to render them love and honor. Hence there was a tendency to the development of individual families, and toward their purity. Where a man had previously married the land, and incidentally obtained a wife, without much thought of a "matrimonial" union, now marriage became moralized, and the natural ties of the individual family the strongest bonds of life. Woman had some choice as to who should be her lord, and ultimately she obtained an entrance into the Feudal hierarchy. She became, somewhat as she had once been, though now on her own account, an object of worship, creating the troubadours and knight-errantry. Her presence softened a bit the rude spirit of warfare, even so much that knights escorting noble ladies were accorded immunity. Yet all was not suddenly become upright and moral. The development of the family was a concomitant, rather than a direct result, of the ideal of Feudalism. Not a few did wrong shamelessly, and many castle walls were witnesses of dark unpublished deeds. But a large number of the clergy, especially bishops, now married openly, and family life was better and more stable than before during the Dark Ages.

<small>Feudal Age</small>

The rule of descent in the family was primogeniture. Some seem to think that this marred the expression of the natural Teutonic idea of justice. Rather it was expressive of the ideal of the age, which gave precedence to position instead of personality. And yet it is true that this was one of the grafts of Rome upon the ideal of the Teutonic nations.

Modern History

Since the fourteenth century there have been sporadic developments of wickedness — in Italy, in England, and in France. They have been, however, the excesses that accompany sudden and great advances in freedom. For a little time, freedom almost invariably degenerates into license. But through all these times of demoralization, in the mainstay of civilization — the middle class — there has been a growth in morality. And the family relationship has increased in stability, as men have come to realize themselves as such, to "take themselves seriously." Yet even here the development is in process. What will ultimately be produced we do not now clearly see. But we believe that there will be, as the final manifestation of the ideal of the present period, a general uprightness of family life, an exaltation of its value and position in the community, and a widespread purity of individual conduct.

CAUSALITY.	THE FAMILY
1 Women not members of tribe,	Corresponds to ideal of warrior.
Reverence to women, sanctity of home, general purity,	To place of family in ideal.
No intermarriage with serfs,	To same; reflex of ideal of personal prowess.
Control and responsibility of father,	To place of family in ideal.
Exposing weak children and aged people,	To ideal as external and physical, *i. e.*, of personal prowess.
Wives by purchase, instead of capture,	To place of family (as a whole) in ideal.
2 Excesses, degeneration,	Due to ideal of personal pleasure.
3 Celibacy of clergy, but only formal; general corruptness,[1]	To ideal of satisfaction of individual, selfish aims.
Royal tutelage,	To same in emperor (though not selfish in bad sense).
Reaction after Charlemagne,	To same in people, showing tendency away from centralization.
4 New impulse to family life,	Reflex of ideal of privilege; also Christian possibly.
Woman has choice in marriage and has entrance into power,	To permeation of ideal of privilege.

---

[1] Remaining of clergy formally unmarried corresponded to the Roman ideal of centralization, obtaining to this extent in the church, but not much, if at all, outside. This is only one instance of many of a kind.

Knight-errantry,	To Christian ideal; and that of privilege.
Primogeniture,	To ideal of privilege.
5 Sporadic wickedness,	Reaction of individual rights; due to ideal of personality, but taking form of gratification of desire for pleasure and of selfish, sensual enjoyment.
Steady growth in family in general,	To ideal of personality.

The primitive Teutonic state was organized on the basis of kin. It was a combination of tribal unity and individual independence. The unit of political life was the freeman, the son of a free father and a free mother. He and his fellows in the family or tribe resided in one community; and assembling in town meeting, they exercised local self-government. Here each man had the right of the initiative, and every one his own separate, unofficial, personal weight. The town meeting was the seat of all legislative and judicial powers. But it might place the latter in the hands of the chiefs, or entrust them to assessors whom it elected. Power was then, as we may infer, dependent on the franchise of the community, and not on kinship or noble blood. The chief was always elected in the village meeting, the degree in which he embodied the qualities enumerated under the ideal being the criterion of his fitness for the position. Should he behave himself unworthily he might be deposed also, as he had been elected. He was not a king, but only a magistrate. It was his business simply to execute the popular will, and so as chief he had no peculiar initiative authority. It was, however, expected that he would extend the boundaries of the tribe and maintain peace. Yet even in war he was mainly a leader. His duty was not so much to issue commands, as to set an example of bravery.

The State— Primitive Teutonic

The single village might extend its domain by conquest, by federation with other communes, or by off-shoot relationships. In such cases, the heads of the whole clan formed together a sort of oligarchy. The chief was simply the highest individual. Yet here also, he was elected by the assembly of the whole tribe. It was the duty of this common moot, as in the single village, to choose the tribal leader and to declare war.

The constitution of these communes shows a tendency, because of the necessities of their life, at one time to democracy and at another to monarchy. The town meetings kept alive the former; local self-government was the rule whenever the nation was at peace. In the assembly, either general or local, every freeman in good standing had a right to a place and a voice. And while in national questions the oligarchy of chiefs might attend to matters of minor importance, all serious affairs were discussed in open meeting. On the other hand, in war the government came near to monarchy. The chief was the supreme leader, followed and obeyed by all the warriors.

In the domain of the judiciary there was the beginning of a legal system. The common test was the ordeal in its different forms, and it was resorted to without regard to class distinctions. The ordinary punishments were death, fines, and mutilations. In general, justice was done, and the wrong-doer received the reward of his crime.

Another feature of the Teutonic commune was its form of land tenure. All the real property of the tribe was apportioned in severalty at stated intervals, and then cultivated for private profit. So both in government and in land-holding there was community, and in the one as in the other the state was strongly democratic. It seems hardly necessary to call attention to it, yet we may notice that each of these features of the early government was expressive of that primitive and rather external ideal which we have already described; an ideal which called for warlike bravery and for personal independence.

Period of Transition

The transitional period was one of influence rather than one of change. Yet, as the ideal assumed a form of more direct gratification of personal desire, we note in the state the confederation of tribes to increase the barbarian power against the Roman arms, and for the invasion of Italy. In the matter of law, the barbarians objected to and would not recognize public law. They kept their own political customs in the midst of the Romans, and every tribe claimed the right to be judged by its own laws. There was, therefore, a gradual merging of public and private law, and ultimately public law was destroyed and rise given to mediæval polity — so strong was the individualistic Teutonic ideal.

Dark Ages

The succeeding centuries (500–1100) marked the elevation of the military chiefs to kingly rulership, and the early elective leadership or monarchy was finally lost in Feudal Europe. It was, among the barbarians, the duty of the victorious chief to divide the booty and the conquered lands among his soldiers. After the invasions there were, therefore, scattered through the newly-acquired territory a number of petty Teuton lords, closely dependent on their king — as, for instance, the soldiers of Odoacer had been in Northern Italy.

Ultimately, by reason of the internal jealousies and the strife which it engendered, this arrangement destroyed full kingship and the possibility of harmony, and free institutions and the political rights of freemen soon disappeared before the greedy appetite of the lords of the land. In 481, Clovis established the Merovingian dynasty in Neustria, and was able, in spite of the efforts of the Austrasian nobility, to develop a considerable dominion. Under Dagobert, however, the more independent of the nobles in Neustria revolted, and the Austrasian Mayors of the Palace became the leaders of Gaul.[1] This decay of the monarchy was followed by another attempt at centralization, likewise personal, *viz.*, the establishment by Charlemagne of the Holy Roman Empire. During his reign it had much power. But by prohibiting national assemblies, while retaining the Frankish lords, he, for the time, put an end to European liberty. When he died the empire practically gave way, and though it continued in West Frankish hands for a century, it was little more than a name. The people generally confounded the power of the dukes as representatives of the central imperial government with their authority as individual lords, and there thus adhered to each duke all whom he could coerce by personal force. Though they had been freemen, the people were soon enslaved, and the struggle was thereafter between the king and the nobles, or among the nobles themselves. In 987, Hugh Capet was able to bring something of order once more out of confusion, but simply by superior power and along the old lines. All France became the private estate of the king. Yet the Capetian monarchy was not anti-Feudal; it was only a return to a sort of unity in the crystallizing Feudal society; hence its strength. Its only great curtailment of

---

[1] Incidentally it may be said that the cause of this defection was the taxes which Dagobert levied for the support of his court. This was contrary to the Teutonic ideas of voluntary service. The Teutons classed taxes and tribute together, therefore their pride was deeply wounded. They were ready to render military service; but they would not pay tribute, when unconquered, and to one whose peers they were.

privileges was the nominal taking away of the right of private war. Meanwhile, in 962, the headship of the Holy Roman Empire had passed to Otto I of Germany. His dominion, too, was essentially personal; and Italy, under a number of petty Feudal lords, was directly subject, more or less, to him.

In this period and in the next, the Roman church was a political party of no mean power. The Holy Roman Empire received its first authority from the pope, as he placed the imperial crown on the brow of Carl the Great. And not a few of its succeeding rulers, both West and East Frankish (German), received coronation at Rome. Likewise in the monarchy of Hugh Capet, the church stood sponsor for the king. He obtained prestige through consecration with the holy oil. He gave protection to the church, and, in turn, the bishops taught obedience to him as a duty. There was close league between church and state. Yet, each sought first its own, and the pope was fully as astute and politic as the emperor.

Roman Church In Politics

The early part (500–700) of this present period, was marked by the codification of the barbarian laws. 506 is the date of the Breviary, the code of Alaric II, which was republished by Charlemagne. The Salic laws were committed to writing somewhat earlier. In 517, appeared the Burgundian code, and in the seventh century the *Leges Visigothorum*. These laws were rather the capitulation of former customs than new enactments. Yet they served for a long time, in conjunction with Roman law, "written reason," as the law of the land. It is characteristic of them, that their regulations are not political, but civil and criminal. So in the Salic law, there are 363 penal to 65 other articles. This code also refers only indirectly to political rights, and that in connection with already established institutions and facts. The Visigothic code is, however, something of an exception. These laws were formulated by the clergy in Spain. Roman influences were naturally quite strong in them, and so the laws are territorial and not personal. In the general mind of Europe, nevertheless, all law was private; and while a distinction might be allowed between public and private law, all that was in force was considered to come under the latter head. In matters of justice, the principal was judgment by one's peers. The ordeal

Legal Matters

was the common judge for slaves, but freemen were allowed simply to swear their innocence. The right of appeal to a higher order was recognized, but the lords preferred the appeal to arms; whence arose private wars.

The year 1100 saw the Feudal system well established, its ideal thenceforth to dominate society for at least three centuries. Sovereignty in this age meant ownership. A suzerain had power over his vassals only when he could compel their action. Government, so far as there was any, was a very loosely confederated group of inharmonious, petty kingdoms. Each baron was a king, at once military leader, ruler, and judge. His power was determined by the number and strength of his vassals, for his position was hereditary, and did not depend on personal prowess. Law was customary, determined by each lord, and different for each suzerainty, and, many times, for each occasion. In these things, moreover, the lord did not confine himself to injuries, or what we ordinarily consider criminal actions, but whatever could possibly be construed as such was crime against him, and served as an excuse for the exhibition of his power. For instance, he held everyone who passed within sight of his castle as in some sense a trespasser, and required from him a tax. *Feudal Age*

Theoretically, Feudalism may have been a rather superior stage of society, but practically it was organized anarchy. To be sure, it had the merit of being nominally entirely voluntary. No man became a vassal without his own consent, and no new conditions could be imposed on him, to which he did not agree. But really, the Feudal organization was a necessity; the weak were compelled to come to the strong and pray, "Defend me, defend me." And the devotion of the vassal extended to whatever might be required of him, and was not at all dependent on the character of his lord. A sample sentiment is this: "My lord, Raoul, is a greater traitor than Judas, but he is my lord. I would not fail him for the world."

In the consideration of this organization of political society, our attention is directed rather to France than to any other division of Europe. But that the ideal of privilege was common to the different parts of the continent, and to England, is shown by the almost universal division into parties struggling upon *Development in France not Solitary* class lines, toward the close of this period. In France, king, clergy, and people, were united against the rapacity of the nobles. In Spain, though a strong free government was never reached, the nobility and the people were pitted against the king. In Germany, progress was slower, but the line was drawn between the emperor, the clergy, and some of the nobility and the majority of the nobility and the people. In England, the nobles and the people early wrested their rights from the king. Magna Charta marks the year 1215, and the first Parliament 1295.[1] Poor Italy was never, until recently, more than half her own, and the church, the communes, the counts and the emperor contested for rulership and for existence.

Two other lines of progress should be briefly traced here, though they are not so much characteristic of this period as they are fore-gleams of the next — the development of law, and that of the communes. It was in the twelfth century that men began to study Justinian's code. In the thirteenth, under Louis IX, the Roman law was translated into French. And the cultivation of these sources and their practical use went hand in hand. For instance, it was in the time of Louis IX, that judicial combats were abolished — a significant fact in Teutonic legal history — and that the right of appeal was broadened from Feudal to royal courts. It is worth remembering, however, that these were only steps in a long process, which had its beginning in the recognition of the code as "written reason" (a fact of which we have already spoken). In the advance there was no scientific selection of laws, or anything like a regular progression. There was simply the gradual assimilation of a principle here, and a maxim there, to the main body of customary law.

Progress in Law

The communes were originally formed from the remains of the old Roman market towns. By tribute, either to the king or to their duke, they purchased immunity from services, and the right of self-government. Nominally, they of course owed over-lordship to some suzerain, but practically they were free,

Development of Communes

---

[1] Coming thus early, it might be questioned whether by their date these do not militate against the theory which we are presenting. But the answer is to be found in the fact of England's isolation. Standing apart from the rest of Europe, her development was less interrupted, and she came more quickly to the possession of the Teutonic birthright.

and so highly did the kings value their support in the contest against the nobles, that, in some instances, they received their charters for some such consideration ; in all cases, they were defended by royalty against the nobility, and, in turn, they maintained the crown. In France, these communities were the ancestors of the *tiers état*. In its essence, each of them was a revolt against the Feudal system. Every city was a sort of close corporation, consisting of a number of guilds. Men were sworn into them as into secret brotherhoods, and to break the oath of loyalty to the commune was a crime of the gravest kind. The rules of the corporations touched even the *minutiæ* of life. Men were allowed to marry whom they might please, only after they had obtained leave from the city. Nor were strangers permitted to obtain a residence. Everyone living within the district of the municipality was compelled to take the communal oath, or answer with his house and goods. In each community, the population was, as outside, divided into estates ; politics was controlled by the merchant guilds. The federation of these cities was a very important feature of communal life. The greatest league was that of the German Hanse, which existed about 1250. It was formed for commercial and political purposes, but was destroyed by jealous discords and by the growth of the great territorial monarchies.

Had it been our object to give in these pages a detailed political history of Europe, the next period, even more than those which have preceded, would require lengthy treatment. Many historians have written bulky volumes upon small portions of it.

Modern History — France

Here, however, we are concerned only to show the general trend of progress, verifying thereby our thesis, and to touch on main and well-known facts. The two political features of the period from 1400 to the present are monarchy and democracy ; and at its first appearance, democracy was the tyranny of the people. In France, in 1500, the prèvotal town was the normal municipality. There was a representative of the king residing there, but the citizens themselves had charge of all internal matters. The town meeting was the legislative authority. The officers of the city were only executive. But in time, owing to outside disorders, and to the creeping in of oligarchy and tyranny, these municipal governments decayed. Another form of measurably free government was that of the provinces *pays d'etats*. These had their origin in normal feudal institutions, but were curtailed by the growth of monarchy, and by the spread of common laws. Nevertheless, they had substantial privileges, and exercised considerable functions, even down to the time of the Revolution. On the other hand, the monarchy was steadily growing. By 1500, feudal opposition to royalty was practically dead. In the Hundred Years War (1339-1453), the monarchy had been crippled far less seriously than Feudalism, and its increasing power was to a large extent the result of this fact. The last great Feudal reaction was in the fifteenth century (1422-1483), when five hundred princes leagued themselves against the king. They were defeated, however, and the kingdom was for some time secure under Louis XI. The place of an oligarchy, partly aristocratic and partly spiritual, was thus taken by a rational, or at any rate, in some sense modern state.

The Revolution was the great crisis of these later centuries, but it was not without its early warnings. There were complaints of abuses many years before it came — and the government seemed willing enough to attend to them. But for some reason, either ignorance or willful neglect, it would never touch the deep and general sources of the evil. Louis XIV added very materially to the unfavorable condition of things, when he changed his landed aristocracy into a court nobility. Heretofore these lords had served as a sort of buffer between the king and the people. But now they were removed; the shock of popular commotion reached the throne; and before long, there was revolution. Unfortunately, however, what was set up on the ruins of the monarchy was an equally unreasonable despotism of the people. From this arose confusion, the Committees, the Terror, and Napoleon. And from this same fact arises to-day, to some extent, the apparent instability of French institutions. Nevertheless, it is more and more evident that these institutions are being gradually moulded by the governing modern ideal of all men as men.

In many ways, France is the center of modern political history, yet the other nations have as truly been concerned in the progressive movement. Germany was almost blotted out in the Thirty

Other Nations — Germany

Years War. In the early part of the seventeenth century, her borders had been full of commerce and industry. But when the war was over, trade and manufacture had gone elsewhere; and they were long in returning. Politically, too, what had been one government became 329 separate domains. Only in the last century has unity arisen, through the aggressiveness of Prussia. And to-day we see for the first time "a Teutonic Empire, on Teutonic soil, composed of Teutonic people, and embodying Teutonic ideas." [1]

England deserves at any rate a moment's attention. As in the years of Restoration, so now, we find her in advance of the continent. Sixteen hund-   *England* red and eighty-eight we may name as the year in which she recovered political and religious liberty. And since that time she has been indeed nominally a monarchy, but practically an aristocratic republic.

The American Revolution should also be mentioned as a part of the politico-social movement. Most marked, perhaps, in France, this came to a   *America* head earlier in America. And it was also really present in other forms in England, unattended by the confusion of war.

It will not be strange if this hurried survey of the political development of Europe not only seems incomplete to the careful student of history, but does not adequately bear out for some minds the problem which we have set ourselves. Different men will place the greatest emphasis on different facts. But if any one will consider in detail the facts of the history of Europe, with the contention of the thesis in mind, we are convinced that he will be simply bringing new material to the support of what we here have been endeavoring to show in outline, the parallel development of the moral ideal of Europe and its political institutions.

	CAUSALITY.	THE STATE
1	Basis of kin, ... Freeman the unit, local self-government, chief only magistrate or leader, delegated authority,	Corresponds to place of family in ideal. To individual independence in ideal.

---

[1] In his "Institutes of General History," President Andrews makes a great deal of this fact, considering it as in a way the culmination of an historical epoch; and it is worthy of more than passing notice from the historical student.

Similar in clan government,	To same.
I. e., Tendency to democracy in peace,	To same.
To monarchy in war,	To ideal of warrior; its reflex.
Justice, fines, ordeal,	To individual independence in ideal.
Community in land-tenure,	To same, which is, of course, a phase of the ideal of personal prowess.
2 Confederation of tribes,	Due to ideal of gain and gratification under warrior type.
Merging of public and private law,	To personal independence in ideal.
3 Military chiefs become kings,	To ideal of personal power; and to working of ideal of man as in political relations.
Petty lords under or without chiefs, various monarchies,	To ideal of personal power and its attainment.
Church in politics,	To same.
Barbarian laws largely civil and criminal,	To ideal of bodily strength and safety, and of satisfaction of individual aims.
Private law,	To satisfaction of individual aims.
Judgment by peers,	To forming ideal of privilege, growing out of personal independence.
Ordeal for slaves only,	To same.
Private wars,	To ideal of satisfaction of individual selfish aims; also to ideal of physical power, force.
3 Sovereignty is ownership, position of lord hereditary,	Due to ideal of privilege.
No confederation, law customary and arbitrary, organized anarchy,	To continuing ideal of satisfaction of individual, selfish aims.
Universal division on class lines into two parties,	To ideal of privilege.
Study and adoption of Justinian's code, broadening of right of appeal, abolition of judicial combats,	To Roman and Christian ideals which had been conserved in the church and were active chiefly there.
Immunity of communes, their federation,	To ideal of privilege; also to ideal of life of labor and trade, conserved in the communes and chiefly active there.
Self-government, brotherhoods, etc.,	To beginning of later ideal, showing in communes in ideal of popular government.
5 Decay and curtailment of free towns and government,	To continuing ideal of privilege.
Monarchy solidified,	To same.
Revolutions,	To ideal of man as man, in political sphere.
Despotisms of the people,	To still continuing ideal of privilege; and to new ideal, being its reflex.
Good republican government by the people,	To ideal of man as man.

Religion— Primitive Teutonic

Once more we go back to the primitive Teutons, and this time to trace the progress in religious ideas and observances. No doubt the early worship was the worship of ancestors, but there were also other divinities. The priesthood, as among the early Greeks, was not the office of a caste, but an avocation of high-born warriors. And by the old custom it fell to the head of the house ; he was its priest. Women, as we have already seen, were considered the representatives, in a sense, of the gods, and their sayings were reverenced and obeyed. Many of the tribes, no doubt, offered human sacrifices. There seems to have been a feeling that the gods demanded the best, and that was life. In similar manner, besides the occasional offering of persons on the altar, men exulted in the sacrifice of themselves in battle, as their highest consecration, and as a means of entrance into the society of the gods.

Odin, Thor, and Freya are typical deities, and as we think of the great hall of the All-Father and of its royal feasts, and of the mighty hammer of the Striker, and of the gentler offices of the goddess of peace, we note their adaptation to a warlike people. And we are also ready to agree with Pfleiderer in marking a "strong tragico-ethical element in Teutonic legends and beliefs."[1]

The Gospel was first preached among the Teutons by missionaries of Arian belief. Aside from doctrinal considerations, the picture of Christ and His twelve chosen followers won their attention, as a form of their own *comitatus* relationship. Therefore they the more readily accepted the teachings of Christianity. And on their own part, they brought to the church, to which they afterward turned from their early Arianism, a purity and vigor which could do much for it as an organization, and a full measure of self-esteem and of assertive power.[2]

<small>Period of Transition</small>

Clovis was the first ruler of the Franks to declare himself a Christian, and thereafter all the Franks were nominally such. About 700, the bishop Boniface, as the representative of the church, labored very earnestly among the Germans, and is said to have baptized 100,000 persons. It was largely through his endeavors that Germany was Christianized ; and those who yet remained unconverted, Charlemagne won over by force.

<small>Dark Ages — "The Centuries of Faith"</small>

It must be borne in mind that it was not simply the mes-

---

[1] See International Journal of Ethics, iii : 1 (Oct. '92), p. 1.

[2] These statements regarding the early influence of Christianity and its adoption by the barbarians do not confine themselves, of course, to the strict chronological limits which we have made. In fact, the seventh century was one of great missionary endeavor among the Northern nations. But the period of transition, which we have elsewhere designated, may for religious institutions be reckoned as the time of the contact of Roman Christianity with the Teutonic tribes, previous to the years when it commenced to work strongly among them

sage of the Cross, and nothing more, to which the barbarians listened. Much as we honor and respect the early heroes of missionary endeavor — and we would not for a moment seem to cast discredit upon their fragrant memory — their zeal for Christianity was mingled with an ardent love for Rome; and along with the vital Christian truth which they faithfully taught, they also inculcated the peculiar teachings of the Roman church. And we may say in passing that the evil influence of many, who bore the name of Christ in the succeeding ages, was the fault, not of the religion which they formally acknowledged, but of the ecclesiastical organization whose representatives they were. Rome claimed the authority to violate all the rights of individuals, and oftentimes, when she had the power, she exercised the asserted prerogative.

Thus it was that in 752-6 the temporal power of the church was asserted. And the reason for this assertion **Temporal Power** was that the popes felt their need of an outward sign to mark their spiritual authority, in order that the church might be on an evident equality with the powers of this world.

The great struggle of the period (500-1100) was that relating to investiture. In the early reigns it had been necessary for the bishops to support the king, in order to obtain the temporal honors which they desired, and to acknowledge him as their temporal superior. Thus they had come to be invested in their sees by him. But the kings soon ceased to let religion govern appointments, and allowed their own friendships to shape their decisions. Moreover, the wealth of the livings of the church appealed to men's cupidity, and young nobles would enter the priesthood for what they could get out of it. Churchly dignities were even sold. The result was a crowd of incumbents who took the profits but left undone the duties of their offices. In the middle of the tenth century the popes and many of the clergy were not by any means a ministry of which to be proud. Debauchery and simony were the commonplaces of papal life and administration. But an improvement in the character of the clergy brought them once more the honor and reverence of their office. The Isidorean or False Decretals were, to a degree, the justification and defence of the papal position; and ultimately, after the experience of Henry at Canossa, the right of investiture was formally surrendered to "God, Sts. Peter and Paul, and the Catholic Church." It is indicative of the power of the church over the people, as well as of the prevalence of ignorance and superstition, that Rome was able to accomplish all these great and far-reaching temporal results, and to subdue even proud and haughty kings, with only anathemas and interdicts as her weapons.

This recognition of papal authority was contemporary with a general cleansing of episcopal life under the direction of Hildebrand, Pope Gregory VII. Ten hundred and eighty-four is the date of the foundation of a new order of monks, the Carthusians, who preached a return to the purity of the rules of Benedict. For thirty years they multiplied in France, Germany, and Italy; and the era of Feudalism began with a church reasonably free from the vices which had previously tainted its life.

<small>Feudal Age — Evil Condition of affairs</small>

But the change was not permanent. The life of the church was in considerable measure of its own times. Intertwined with the Feudal system in the extension and increase of her temporal power, she also partook of its evils, of anarchy and of laxity. Most marked was the latter. The vicious results of the teaching of sacerdotal celibacy were fearful in this period, and the evil which might be wrought through the confessional rose to its greatest height. Nor were the clergy at pains to conceal their vices. In the middle of the thirteenth century, Pope Alexander IV declared that the "people are positively corrupted by their pastors," who by their own looseness stimulated the already too common laxity of principle. And the popular mind instinctively assumed the immoralities of those who should have furnished it instruction in the paths of righteousness. There seems to have been some improvement for a time, but only that the evil might burst out again; and the lull was due rather to restraint than to desire to escape from sin.

A century later, at the time of the Renaissance, there was this same unpleasant sight in Italy. Men made much of the hierarchy, and religious feeling was so strong that the first expressions of the new artistic style were limited to architecture, for fear of the stigma of heterodoxy. Yet there was apparently very little connection between the teachings of the Scriptures

<small>In Italy at the Time of the Renaissance</small>

and men's daily lives. Even the clergy were notoriously profligate. Then the movement spread to the domain of religious thought. So pagan did it become that men talked openly of leaving the church for Mohammedanism, and prophesied the speedy downfall of Christianity. And, humanly speaking, we are surprised that their prediction was not verified. Conservatives were driven to denounce Plato, Averroes, and Alexander of Aphrodisia as the three pests of Italy.

The condition of things in Italy was, fortunately, an exaggeration of what befel the rest of papal Europe. **Other Developments in the Rest of Europe** In other countries, there were contemporary facts which promised much more for the future.

One was the founding of the mendicant orders, from 1216 to 1256, a new means for the propagation of Christian and papal teachings. Another was the accessibility of holy orders, all classes and talents being received. Anyone might enter the service of the church — though she denied the right of private judgment, and assumed the authority to compel obedience. A third fact, strongly in contrast with this compulsion, was the openness of ecclesiastical discussion and the frequency of church councils.

It is evident from the strongly rationalistic turn of thought in Italy, and in general may be inferred from **Modern History — The Reformation** the fact that the Renaissance, spreading to other countries, must ultimately have its effect upon religious authority all over Europe, that the papal power was being slowly undermined. The rise of Scholasticism, and of men like Abelard, who would not be coerced, and the prevalence of free inquiry both within and outside the schools, boded ill for a despotic power. The Roman Church was the crystallization of the Roman ideal with few Teutonic elements. The new life, conversely, was to be governed by the Teutonic ideal, with a decreasing number of Roman elements.

It was in the dawning of such an era that Wyclif came preaching in England, in the latter half of the fourteenth century. And when his enemies, in defiance, cast his ashes to the waves, they only, to the poet's mind, supplied the physical conditions, which had already their spiritual and intellectual counterpart, for a movement that should be bounded only by the limits of the seas.

Then Huss and Jerome of Prague arose, and on the other side, the awful tortures of the Inquisition were brought into play. We see, on the one hand, the lessening of the papal power, the decay of Christian observances, the viciousness of a ruling clergy, and the horrors of a rack which only faith could defy; and on the other, the growth of freedom of religious thought, the inspiration of life with vital Christianity, a purity of walk in the hero-reformers which shines with glorious brilliancy, and beyond, the crown of martyrdom, the reward of unfaltering confession. Who can doubt which will conquer?

The fire smoulders on, and Tetzel comes to Germany to sell indulgences. Luther is aroused, and in a moment of righteous indignation nails his *theses* to the door in Wittemburg. Instantly the smouldering fire is aflame. Hatred to Rome grows hotter and infects all the people. The Bible is given out in the German vernacular, and one chain of the bondage is broken forever. Behind Luther was the intelligence and the moral earnestness of the German people, and they, not he, made the breach with Rome.

But that which they desired, they did not obtain. Only after much difficulty was the emperor, who was the head, we remember, of the Holy Roman Empire, forced to consent to freedom of religious belief, and the result, then, was not complete freedom, but the Lutheran church. It was only after the Thirty Years War that the question of German religious liberty was settled. Really there was little distinction made between truth and the form in which truth was held. None the less, there was throughout these movements of the Renaissance and the Reformation a great change in general religious belief. "Consciences were freer and devotion was more real and spiritual. Life was looked on as in itself worth living, and religion as more a personal than a collective matter."

In England, it was Henry VIII who, for reasons rather bad than good, took the first step in breaking away from Rome. But it was left for the Independents to complete his beginning, and to vindicate religious liberty in the colony at Plymouth Rock. That handful has leavened the new world; and those who remained behind at home were the nucleus of an increasing number who, with varying fortune but with growing success,

The Movement Outside Germany

are still laboring for disestablishment in Britain. In France, also, the work is not complete, nor has it progressed so far. Under Philip the Fair papacy fell, and with it, its supporters, the Templars. But because he had lost control of the king, the pope did not forsake the people. To-day France is a Roman Catholic country, and the power of an ecclesiastical hierarchy is dominant. But the Gallican church and the preaching of Pere Hyacinthe are the protest of a slowly awakening consciousness of the right of religious freedom.

	CAUSALITY.	RELIGION
1	Worship of ancestors,	Corresponds to place of family in ideal.
	The head of the family is the priest,	To same.
	Typical divinities,	To warrior ideal.
	Human sacrifices,	To warrior (physical) ideal.
2	Power of story of Christ and the twelve disciples,	Due to warrior ideal, and its manifestation in the *comitatus*.
3	Missionary work ; by missionaries,	Due to Christian ideal.
	by emperor,	To ideal of satisfaction of personal aims, and force.
	Temporal power of church and her violation of individual rights,	To satisfaction of personal aims.
	Degradation of Investiture,	To same.
	Corruptness in church,	To satisfaction of selfish aims.
	Struggle about Investiture was between two parties, each animated	By same ideal of satisfaction of personal aims, though on side of the church there was a deeper element.
4	Purity at beginning of Feudal Age,	To Christian ideal.
	Laxity and evil,	To same as in preceding ; also to ideal of privilege as making the clergy members of a class, and so secure, instead of being so many individual messengers of the Cross.
	Mendicant orders,	To Christian ideal. (Wholly ?)
	Accessibility of holy orders, and openness of ecclesiastical discussion,	To same ; also remaining, inherited from the early church.
5	Reformation,	To ideal of man as man, in religious affairs.
	Opposition to Reformation,	To preceding ideals.
	Pilgrims, Disestablishment, and other similar movements,	To ideal of man as man.

Class Distinctions and Slavery — Primitive Teutonic

In early Teutonic society the only rigid class division was that between free and unfree. Yet among those who were free, the men who were honored with high positions as chiefs, or with membership in the *comitatus* of a chief, might be termed nobles. Their dignity, however, carried with it no especial political privileges. It is quite evident that the Teutons did not regard blood and rank as convertible terms ; and so, in the official nobility of the *comitatus*, it was bravery and personal prowess alone that were the marks of distinguishing excellence. Among these people slavery lacked the harsh sting which it possessed among the Greeks and Romans. It was not a vital part of the Teutonic organization, but rather an accident of the Teutonic state. To them a slave was not an animal or an agricultural "instrument," but a man who lacked certain privileges, and so there was no elaborate cruelty exercised toward him. Slaves might, it is true, have been killed in a fit of anger, but the same was true of freemen. They were allowed to live in their own houses as men, and in some measure of domesticity. Yet, on the other hand, if possible, the Germans sold their slaves, and there was no strong sentiment against any treatment of them. Slaves were distinguished from freemen by short hair. Freemen wore theirs long, and there were regulations to maintain this distinction. Originally, probably, slaves were captives taken in war, but later they were the result of marriage, of debt (incurred by gambling), or of poverty.

In the short time of the first contact with Rome, the barbarians saw uses for slaves of which, perhaps, they had had no idea, and the result was that those who had it in their power proceeded to follow the fresh examples of selfish enjoyment, with the aid of all their slaves. Yet this did not last long, for society was too disintegrated in Western Europe for any such thing as luxury. The form which it finally took was that of making others till the soil, while the lord attended to matters of war and pleasure.

<small>Period of Transition</small>

In the early part of this period (500–1100), freemen were divided into kings, nobles, and free-holders. How freemen were ranked, the wergild gives an idea. By Salic law, the fine imposed for the murder of a nobleman was 600 *solidi* ; of a Roman who had been admitted to the royal table, 300 ; of a common Frank, 200 ; of an ordinary Roman land-holder, 100 ; of a person who cultivated the property of another, 45. By the ninth century, land-holding had come to be the important test, and the classes were lords, vassals, and under them, vavassors. Peasants who commended themselves were still called free. But how essential the possession of property was may be judged from the fact that no man who was not a free-holder could testify against

<small>Dark Ages</small>

(*i. e.*, judge) a freeman. In this society there were two estates, the nobility and the clergy. The latter bore their peculiar mark of the tonsure. They had a great deal of power, and not only were they commonly reverenced, but ultimately, they secured freedom from civil justice and authority. The laity below the nobility were classed according to the way in which they held their land, as well as by the steps of vassalage. There were first, allodial holders, who rendered their lords general homage. There were next, the proprietors of benefices, who were dependent on the one from whom they held the land. The third class consisted of the occupants of tributary lands, who paid rents and services. And last were the serfs who were attached to the soil (including the Fiscalins, who worked for the support of the emperor).

With regard to the position of the slaves, these menials had been somewhat elevated. They were now, in the eleventh century, not mere chattels, but serfs attached to the soil. For this change, the church deserves not a little credit. In England, however, there was a regular slave trade with Ireland, from 1066 till the time of Henry II, when it came to an end by reason of a non-importation compact to which the Irish were willing to agree. In Italy the Venetians carried on a similar trade with Oriental countries for the luxuries which they could thus obtain; but this is part and parcel of the old Italian selfishness, and not the record of the Teutonic ideal.

In the Feudal epoch, four things of which we have already spoken, yet three of them bearing strongly the marks of the Age, prepared the destruction of the distinctions of caste. Feudal social order itself was, without exception, one hierarchy of landed possession. The upper classes fought and feasted, while the lower worked and suffered. But, on the other hand, these four vital forces were at work. The first was the church. By its policy of receiving whoever might come, whether bond or free, it tended to break up both caste distinction among the free-born, and the institution of slavery itself. Next were the crusades, the glory of proclaiming which belonged to the church, but which had results far beyond what the church anticipated. A serf was freed on crusading. So he and his lord became better acquainted, and a sort of fraternal feeling arose. The consequence was mutually truer and higher esteem, and there followed, too, extensive emancipation at home. Another unlooked-for result was the death of many large proprietors away from home, and the consequent dismemberment of their fiefs. This worked for the destruction of class distinctions among those who were free. In the third place, the rise of commerce brought new arts and abilities into demand, and those who were able to furnish them, no matter who they were, rose in the social scale. Particularly does this apply to the communes. The aid which they received in this way was very great. In these cities were found practically, all the legal learning, technical skill, and business enterprise, and much of the ability and patriotism of Europe. They were the hope of the future society. The fourth influence was that of the study of the Justinian code. As a result of this, in 1256, Bologna gave freedom to all within her walls. Louis VII (1137–80) had made a similar enactment for France, and Louis X, in 1315, did likewise. In England, Edward I, in 1295, quoting from the code, declared that "according to the rights of nature, everyone should be born free." In the case of England, this at once freed all the serfs on the royal domains; and it worked on gradually till serfdom was finally given up, free labor being also found to be more profitable. The serfs became tenants under contract, and voluntary services took the place of the old servitudes.

In the latest stage, in modern history, there has been a gradual and more perfect freeing from the ideal of class distinctions. Yet it has come very slowly, and its most marked developments have been within the limits of almost the last one hundred years. In France in the eighteenth century, the nobility had no relation to their tenants. They looked on them as only producers, and considered themselves immeasurably above them. But the French Revolution, which was chiefly a social rebellion, changed this. For, aside from the overturning which it produced, the larger number of the nobility emigrated, almost at the commencement of the trouble. In England, since the seventeenth century, the tendency has been to vertical rather than horizontal divisions, to distinctions on political rather than on social lines. And the same thing is true to a much larger extent in

Modern History

the United States. In both England and America, in France and in Germany as well, the great problem to-day is what men call the labor problem, the question of social adjustment. Yet, as will readily be perceived, its aspect is somewhat changed, and the question is by no means altogether one of rank. While the deference which wealth receives is not small, there is still a large portion of praise and esteem for a man who is simply and truly a man.

CAUSALITY.   CLASS DISTINCTIONS AND SLAVERY

1. Official *comitatus* nobility, . . Corresponds to warrior ideal.
   Slavery of certain classes of persons, Reflex of same ideal.
   Good treatment in main, . . To lack of class spirit in ideal.
2. Slaves made to do all the work, . Due to ideal of personal pleasure.
3. Kings, nobles, and free-holders, . Remaining from early distinctions and therefore due to that ideal; also to ideal of satisfaction of personal aims.

   Distinctions based on land holding, To growing ideal of privilege, based on ideal of satisfaction of personal aims.

   Slaves become serfs attached to the soil, ... To working of Christian ideal.
4. Hierarchy of landed possession, . Due to ideal of privilege.
   Introduction of voluntary services, To growing ideal of following period, and to still remaining satisfaction of individual aims.
5. French revolution, political rather than social divisions, abolition of slavery, labor problem, . . To ideal of man as man.

Other Social Customs — Early Teutonic

A few other social customs may briefly come before us. In keeping with the barbaric society of early times were the amusements in which the Teutons indulged. Some of the tribes were particularly given to gluttony. All of them seem also to have had an instinctive hospitality; anyone might stay as a guest for three nights. "Banquets and hospitality," wrote Tacitus, "find such favor as in no other nation." During or after the feast, it was the custom for minstrels to sing songs of the battle, and such as were calculated to incite the warriors to noble deeds. Another "after-dinner" custom was that called "flytting," consisting chiefly in the making of taunting and cutting remarks with impunity. There was also, at this time, a great amount of personal boasting.

The most besetting vice of the Teuton was gambling. Everybody gambled, old and young, women as well as men. People staked all their possessions, and then, oftentimes, themselves. And thus it came about that many slaves had been free-born members of the tribe. To the credit, however, of all these men and women be it said, that they were honorable in the discharge of their obligations ; they paid their debts.

Another typical custom was that of blood brotherhood, in which, by the mingling of their blood, two men of different families became brothers. With this, as with all other blood relationship, there went, first, the notion of mutual peace, and second, the avenging of injuries to blood relations. Some think that the wergild was devised to meet these cases, so great confusion did the feuds due to blood relationship bring on ; and the same may easily be true of the ordeal.

Still another custom, and one of great importance to the future warrior, was "the gift of arms." This took place at ages varying from 12 to 21, usually about 15. It was the formal recognition that the youth was no longer a boy, but one who might be called on to defend the tribe.

Regarding the period from 500 to 1100, we have already noted its intense individualization, and the expression of this in the prevalence of private war. **Dark Ages** Another fact peculiarly illustrative of this characteristic temper, is the local nature of institutions and arrangements of all kinds. No two suzerains ordained similar customs in any matter, except by accident. Another significant fact is the number of men who went into monasteries, and of women who sought the solitude of convent life. Whatever we may think of this as a mark of religious zeal, we can agree with Kingsley that it might have been only the use of common sense, and done to escape the rack and ruin of the Dark Ages. And we may add still further our own idea, that in its seeking for comfort and rest for self, it marks that giving up to personal ends which characterized all life of this trying age.

The great institution of Feudal times on which we have not touched as yet is Chivalry. In explanation it goes back to the customs of private **Feudal Age — Chivalry** war. So disastrous did these feuds become, that, in 1041, the pope declared the Truce of God. By its provisions there was to be no private warfare between Wednesday night and Monday morning. At first, it decreed universal peace between these times ; but that could not be maintained. The truce, however, did considerable good, though the evil was by no means remedied. Kings and lords showed their approval of the plan — for other people, by declaring various truces on their domains. But they were evidently all only restraints. The ideal did not change; instead, it simply sought new fields. So, many went to Sicily; 60,000 went to England with William of Normandy in 1066. Then came the pilgrimages which the church proposed, and the Crusades. But, after a time, something else had to be devised, and this something appeared in the tournaments of Chivalry. They took the place of the excitements of private warfare, and blended with them the interests of religion and gallantry. In reality, Chivalry, which we commonly restrict to these latter, had to do with the Crusades as well. Gautier tells us that it "was at first primarily religious, turning to Jerusalem long before the Crusades. But," he adds, "the Cycle of Arthur and the Round Table changed the character to a more effeminate type. The result has been in modern times a wrong idea of Chivalry." This evidently covers the whole extent of knighthood in Europe. So far as what we are saying is concerned, it serves to bring out in stronger fashion the religious basis of Chivalry. And, in fact, the duties and purposes of the knight were of no mean character. From the Rules of Chivalry,[1] we can see that under the dominant ideal of privilege there was much that was good and pure and true.

Thus, while men fought for preferment, and boasted of the glory of the place which they won in the lists, or of the enemies of the church whom they had vanquished, we note that their desire for victory had been enlisted under the banner of what is good and true. And yet this was all simply a taking mode proposed by the church, partly with a genuine social purpose, and

---

[1] These are the ten commandments of the knight:
1 Thou shalt believe all that the church teaches, and shalt observe all its directions.
2 Thou shalt defend the church.
3 Thou shalt respect all weaknesses, and shall constitute thyself the defender of them.
4 Thou shalt love the country in which thou wast born.
5 Thou shalt not recoil before thine enemy.
6 Thou shalt make war against the infidel without cessation and without mercy.
7 Thou shalt perform scrupulously thy feudal duties, if they be not contrary to the laws of God.
8 Thou shalt never lie, and shalt remain faithful to thy pledged word.
9 Thou shalt be generous and give *largesse* to everyone.
10 Thou shalt be everywhere and always the champion of the right and the good against injustice and evil.

partly with a view to the continuance of its own supremacy — a mode for the expression of the still active ideal of the attainment of individual ends, and for the display of the feudal ideal of privilege.

In our own day there is one social institution, and we will not stop to name others, in the waning of which may be seen the growth of the modern ideal of personality. It is that of the court life as the rule and example for the country.   *Modern Times* In two cases, those of America and France, this is not true to-day. There is a certain community of social institutions, at any rate in the former, among all classes of educated people. And while, on the other hand, the English people, for instance, care much for the Queen and the court, there are some signs of the breaking down of the royal prestige there also.

	CAUSALITY.	OTHER SOCIAL CUSTOMS
1	Banquets and gluttony,	Corresponding to ideal of warrior as a physical ideal.
	Bards, flytting, boasting of deeds, blood-brotherhood, gift of arms,	To warrior ideal.
	Paying debts,	To ideal of uprightness.
	Gambling,	(Seems to correspond with the recklessness of a warrior ideal.)
2, 3	Private wars,	Due to ideal of satisfaction of individual aims.
	Local institutions and arrangements,	To the same.
	Many seeking monasteries and convents,	To satisfaction of personal ends; also to a Christian ideal.
4	Truce of God as a restraint,	To continuing ideal of satisfaction of personal aims.
	Chivalry,	To Christian ideal, in part.
	As only for nobility,	To ideal of privilege.
5	Waning of power of example of court life,	To ideal of man as man, still increasing.

IV — PARALLEL DEVELOPMENT OF INSTITUTIONS RELATING TO INDIVIDUAL CULTURE

There remain the customs of education, and in them also we may trace a development parallel to that of the ideal. Among the Teutons, the rule was ignorance. Writing, so far as there was any,   *Primitive Teutonic* was considered to be woman's work — and this was the popular sentiment of Europe all through the Middle Ages. In the barbarian boys, the chief thing that was sought was hardihood and courage. Their training was physical and martial. We find them forbidden to weep or cry aloud under penalty of death by drowning; and we are told that their whole education might appropriately be summed up in the learning of one lesson, *De contemnenda morte.*

In the period from 500 to 1100, Charlemagne made a serious effort to establish common education. So strong were his ideas on this matter that some maintain that his reign, could it have been continued, would have been the beginning of modern history. He instructed the clergy, who were the only learned class, to take care of the education of the people and of the reviving of literature and the arts. And in order to this, he admonished the ecclesiastics themselves to resume their studies, with which the social confusion had seriously interfered. These reforms, however, were not very widespread, nor were they stable. Affairs were still in too great turmoil for scholarship, and the people cared but little for knowledge. Soon after Charlemagne's time, even the clergy returned to their own ways. For instance, a collection of German songs, which he had made, was declared an ungodly book and ordered destroyed.

[500–1100]

In the years 900–1100, however, there was the beginning of the Scholastic movement, which was really the conserver of intellectual activity down to modern times. By the ingenuity of its fantastic speculations, if by nothing else, it served to keep alive the philosophic instinct of Europe.

In educational matters, the great advance of this time was that commonly known as the University Movement. In 1150, Oxford and Bologna were founded; 1200 is the date of the universities of Paris and Salamanca. Yet here, the continual scholastic quibblings are typical of the age, and the ideal of privilege made a great deal of trouble, as it did in politics. We must not make the mistake of thinking that there was at this time a pure and genuine literary interest. It was not till the demand was made, not by the voice of one man, or by the desire of a few, but by the needs of all, that there was a revival of letters. There was little love of literature for its own sake. The zeal was rather to transform pagan works for Christian uses, as the palimpsests testify; or to destroy them altogether, as works of the devil. Yet it is in this age that we have the rise of poetry

[1100–1400]

and of the modern theater, as well as of the universities. Scholasticism continued till after 1600, but it received its death blow from Bacon and Descartes. Slowly, but surely, the principle of observation took the place of its sophistic reasonings.

In the instruction of children, in each of these ages, the aim was to make men such as their fathers were. In the Dark Ages after Charlemagne there was no study or learning, except in the monasteries; and we can imagine how the boy was trained to his father's place, and had no ambition for anything more. If the story of the young Alfred learning to read is a picture of education in the palace, what was it in the country outside? In the period of Feudalism the same was true, save for the growing intelligence of the dwellers in the Free Cities. The Crusades, however, stimulated the minds of those who fought for the Holy Sepulchre, and a number of influences conspired to cause an intellectual awakening. Now it was that the work of the Universities and of the monasteries began to show, and it was the sparks which they had kindled that burst forth into the brilliant discoveries of Copernicus and Christopher Columbus.

<small>Instruction 500—1400</small>

The new ideal of man as man, which was the gradual outgrowth of the old age of Feudal Europe, has in modern times been accompanied by a most marvelous advance in learning and in common education. Where one or two were acquainted with the elementary branches, now scores and even hundreds and thousands have passed far beyond them: and where men only were trained in intellectual matters, now the education of women and co-education are the rule. The state, by the establishment of public schools and universities, has been able to offer to everyone the opportunity of intellectual improvement.

<small>Modern Education</small>

The specializations of manual and scientific training for particular vocations, instead of a general culture preparatory for life, mark one extreme of the educational tendency. It does not seem, however, to be a final stage. For the number of people who recognize the value of a thorough education in any walk of life is constantly increasing, and it is being recruited in part from the ranks of those very specialists. Yet the other idea must run its course. Not before then, in matters of education, can we approximate to the ideal of symmetrical development, the dream of Froebel — an all-round man.

	CAUSALITY.	EDUCATION
1	Physical and martial, *De contemnenda morte*,	Corresponds to warrior ideal.
	Writing given over to women,	To same.
2	Instability of Charlemagne's innovations,	Due to ideal of satisfaction of individual selfish aims.
3 and 4	Boy to be like father,	To working of ideal of privilege.
	Scholasticism,	To ideal of privilege, as intended to prove the truth of its positions.
	Scholastic quibbles,	To continuing ideal of individual satisfaction.
4	Growing intelligence in Free Cities, University movement,	To early growth of new ideal.
5	Revival of learning,	To ideal of man as man, in intellectual matters.
	Principle of observation,	Of every man as man.
	Common education, of men and women,	To same.
	Kindergarten,	Of person as person, in fullest sense.
	Specialization,	To same, in its extreme in the individual.

For Summary, see following chart:

of education, can we approximate to the ideal of symmetrical development, the dream of Froebel — an all-round man.

	CAUSALITY.	EDUCATION
1	Physical and martial, *De contemnenda morte*,	Corresponds to warrior ideal.
	Writing given over to women,	To same.
2	Instability of Charlemagne's innovations,	Due to ideal of satisfaction of individual selfish aims.
3 and 4	Boy to be like father,	To working of ideal of privilege.
	Scholasticism,	To ideal of privilege, as intended to prove the truth of its positions.
	Scholastic quibbles,	To continuing ideal of individual satisfaction.
4	Growing intelligence in Free Cities,	To early growth of new ideal.
	University movement,	
5	Revival of learning,	To ideal of man as man, in intellectual matters.
	Principle of observation,	Of every man as man.
	Common education, of men and women,	To same.
	Kindergarten,	Of person as person, in fullest sense.
	Specialization,	To same, in its extreme in the individual.

For Summary, see following chart:

CHART OF TEUTONIC IDEALS AND INSTITUTIONS

PERIOD	IDEAL	INSTITUTIONS							INDIVIDUAL CULTURE
		SUBJUGATION OF NATURE		SOCIAL	RELATING TO				
		Material Welfare	Common Occupation	Family	ORGANIZATION				
					State	Religion	Social Customs	Education	
Primitive Teutonic —400 A.D.	Warrior. Personal prowess and independence. Fidelity, courage, purity. External.	Home; some comfort, little luxury.	War, hunting, work of smith. Little commerce. Women and slaves do farm and home work; also writing(?), cobbling, and tailoring.	Woman sacred; man's equal in courage and morality; his superior in wisdom and prudence. Marriage sacred; household also. Little sentiment in marriage. Purity of life. No late marriage between slaves and freemen.	On basis of kin; freeman the unit; local self-government; chief only the executive and leader. Power dependent on franchise of community. Community of lands. Justice by ordeal.	Worship of ancestors; also gods. No priestly caste. Human sacrifices. Strong imitative-ethical element.	Caste—Free and unfree. Comitatus nobility. Bravery the criterion, not blood. Slavery—An accident. Treatment not harsh. Custom—Hospitality; some gluttony; uxoriousness; "fysting"; and boasting; gambling; paid their debts; blood-brotherhood; "gift of arms."	General intellectual ignorance. Writing (?) for women. Physical and martial. Object: Hardihood and courage. Lesson: De contemnenda morte.	
Roman-Teutonic—Transitional 400–900 (circum.)	Warrior, and Personal Gratification. Yet man in political relations. External (Influence rather than change.)	Reveling in Roman luxury.	War. Pleasure-making.	Degeneration in morality. Yielding to corrupting influences of Italy.	Confederation of tribes. "Personality of law."	Preaching of Christianity by Arian and Roman missionaries.	Increase in number of slaves; set to tilling the soil.	In general the same.	
Dark Ages 900–1100	Satisfaction of Selfish Aims. Individualistic. External.	General rudeness and poverty.	Feud and revenge for all who have the power. Agriculture for serfs and others who are driven to it.	Corruption. Celibacy of clergy works harm. Celibacy more important than purity.	Individual attempts at centralization by the Merovingians, (Holy Roman Empire) by Charlemagne and by Hugh Capet. Growing power of church. All law in force considered to be private; judgment by peers; ordeal for slaves. Private wars.	Growth of papacy. Assertion of temporal power and struggle over investiture; right finally given up to the church. Debauchery and simony among clergy.	Estates—King, nobles, and clergy. Also freeholders; land-owners. Lords, vassal, and vavassors. Slavery—Slaves raised to serfs attached to the soil. Custom—All institutions local. Many flee to monasteries and convents.	General aim: To make children like fathers. Affairs is too great confusion for scholarship, although Charlemagne advocated it. People did not care. Beginning of scholasticism.	
Restoration of Order—Feudalism 1100–1400	Privilege and Position. Individualistic. Ambition for power. Personal rights. Truth-speaking; liberality; frankness. External. Latent: In communes; popular government and a life of labor and trade. In church: equality and social unity.	Feudal castle. Some luxury, but no elegance. Wretchedness among peasants.	Warfare. Crusades. Dueling of armorers. Rise of commerce and manufactures. Restrictions of guilds and corporations.	Greater purity. Higher thought of marriage. Knight-errantry. Many clergy marry openly. Primogeniture.	Feudal system. All forms and actions local and occasional. Law customary. Division generally into two political parties which struggle for rights and power. Study of law. Judicial combats abolished. Communes; each a revolt against Feudalism.	Evils of Feudalism in church; depravity among clergy; restricted somewhat. Mendicant orders. Accessibility of holy orders. Openness of ecclesiastical discussion.	Caste—Hierarchy of landed possession. Working for its destruction were extensibility of churchly orders, crusades, rise of commerce, study of Justinian code. Slavery—Many serfs freed in England. Serfs in other countries become tenants under contract. Custom—Chivalry; at first, religious; later, light, to gallantry.	Scholasticism. University movement. Rise of poetry and modern charter. Good work in monasteries. General aim much the same as in last period. Growth of principle of observation.	
Revolution and Readjustment; Modern Times 1400–	Man as Man. Conscious realization of personality in intellectual, religious, political, and social affairs. A person as a person. Self-conscious.	Broader diffusion of movable wealth. Inventions and discoveries. French Revolution allowed greater material welfare; progress in this line most prominent. Modern discoveries.	Developments in number of occupations. Division of labor. Freedom of labor and trade.	Sporadic immorality. In general, growth of morality. Increased stability of and respect for family relation.	Establishment of constitutionalism, i. e., monarchy, and a government by the people, i. e., democracies and republics.	The Reformation. Religion more a personal than a collective concern. English Reformation. Independents. Progress of Disestablishment in Britain. Gallican church in France.	Caste—French Revolution a social revolution. Division on political rather than social lines. Great question today, that of social adjustment. Slavery—General abolition of slavery. Custom—Waning of power of court over common life.	Renaissance. Advance in learning. Common and public education. Education of women. Technical education. Kindergarten.	

CONCLUSION

A few words by way of conclusion to what has been said in these pages. History, on the face of things, has been dealt with in a most cursory way. But the aim has not been to rewrite the facts. Rather we have hoped to show that history is moral; that it has a living moral inwardness, just as our conduct has to-day; that institutions have, historically, a moral side, and a moral reason for their existence; and that, in fact, the true history is not in what institutions present, so much as in what they manifest.

AUTHORITIES

METAPHYSICAL

Alexander	Moral Order and Progress
Aristotle	Nichomachean Ethics
	Politics
Bluntschli	Theory of the State
Comte	Positive Philosophy
Conway	Morality of Nations
Dewey	Principles of Ethics
Erdmann	History of Philosophy
Green	Prolegomena to Ethics
Harris	Hegel's Logic
Hegel	Philosophy of History
Jodl	Geschichte der Ethik
Kedney	Hegel's Aesthetics
Lieber	Political Ethics
Lotze	Microcosmus
Mackenzie	Social Philosophy
Maurice	Social Morality
Muirhead	Elements of Ethics
Schurman	Ethical Import of Darwinism
Spencer	Data of Ethics
	Politics
	Sociology
Stephen	Science of Ethics

HISTORICAL

General

Andrews	Institutes of General History
Brace	Gesta Christi
Eliot	Liberty of Nations
Encyclopaedias	Britannica
	International
Erdmann	History of Philosophy
Geffcken	Church and State
Labberton	Outlines of History
Mann, H.	Ancient and Mediæval Republics
Seaman	Progress of Nations
Wickoff	Four Civilizations of the World
Willson	Outlines of History
Wilson, Woodrow	The State

Greece

Benn	The Greek Philosophers
Burnet	Early Greek Philosophy
Duruy	History of Greece
Davies, J.	Hesiod and Theognis
Dyer	Greek Religion
Eschenburg	Manual of Classical Literature
Felton	Greece, Ancient and Modern
Gardner, Percy	New Chapters in Greek History
Grant	Ethics of Aristotle
Grote	History of Greece
Guhl and Koner	The Life of the Greeks and Romans. (Also Rome)
Herodotus	Works (Cary)
Homer	Iliad. (Lord Derby's translation)
Macy	Hellenica

Mahaffy	Old Greek Life
	Old Greek Education
	Social Life in Greece
	Greek Life and Thought
	Greek World under Roman Sway
	Problems in Greek History
Perry	History of Greek Literature
Schliemann	Records of Various Excavations
Smith, William	History of Greece
	Classical Dictionary
Taylor, T.	The Eleusinian and Bacchic Mysteries
Thucydides	
Verschoyle	Ancient Civilization. (Also Rome)
Zeller	Outlines of Greek Philosophy

Rome

Becker	Gallus
Bury	Later Roman Empire
Cicero	
Church	Roman Education
Duruy	History of Rome
Farrar	Darkness and Dawn
Gibbon	Decline and Fall of the Roman Empire
Hatch	Organization of the Early Christian Churches
Horace	Odes. (MacLeane's ed.)
Inge	Roman Society under the Caesars
Juvenal	Satires
Livy	
Mommsen	History of Rome
Montesquieu	Grandeur and Decadence of the Romans
Niebuhr	Rome
Plutarch	Lives
Polybius	
Seeley	Roman Imperialism
Seneca	Essays
Smith, William	History of Rome
Uhlhorn	Conflict of Christianity with Heathenism

The Teutons

Bryce	Holy Roman Empire
Duruy	History of the Middle Ages
Emerton	Introduction to the Middle Ages
Guizot	History of Civilization in Europe
Gautier	Chivalry
Gummere	Germanic Origins
Hallam	Middle Ages
Kaufmann	Socialism and Communism in their Practical Application
Kingsley	The Roman and the Teuton
Lecky	Development of European Morals
Lea	Sacerdotal Celibacy
Maine	Village Communities
Martin, Henri	Histoire de France
Milman	History of Latin Christianity
Müller	Political History of the 19th Century
Smith, T.	Mediæval Missions
Storrs	Bernard of Clairvaux
Tacitus	Germania
Verschoyle	Modern Civilization
West	Alcuin

Also

Huth	Marriage of Near Kin
Manley	Woman outside Christendom
Thwing	The Family

IDEALS AND INSTITUTIONS THEIR PARALLEL DEVELOPMENT

JOHN ERNEST MERRILL

www.ingramcontent.com/pod-product-compliance
Lightning Source LLC
Chambersburg PA
CBHW020254170426
43202CB00008B/359